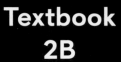

Textbook
2B

Maths — No Problem!

Singapore Maths
English National Curriculum 2014

Consultant and Author
Dr. Yeap Ban Har

UK Consultant
Dr. Anne Hermanson

Authors
Dr. Foong Pui Yee
Lim Li Gek Pearlyn
Wong Oon Hua

shinglee

Published by Maths — No Problem!
Copyright © 2016 by Maths — No Problem!

Printed in the United Kingdom
First Printing, 2015
Reprinted twice in 2015 and twice in 2016

ISBN 978-1-910504-08-6

Maths — No Problem!
Dowding House, Coach & Horses Passage
Tunbridge Wells, UK TN2 5NP
www.mathsnoproblem.co.uk

Acknowledgements

This Maths — No Problem! series, adapted from the New Syllabus
Primary Mathematics series, is published in collaboration with
Shing Lee Publishers. Pte Ltd.

Design and Illustration by Kin

Preface

Maths — No Problem! is a comprehensive series that adopts a spiral design with carefully built-up mathematical concepts and processes adapted from the maths mastery approaches used in Singapore. The Concrete-Pictorial-Abstract (C-P-A) approach forms an integral part of the learning process through the materials developed for this series.

Maths — No Problem! incorporates the use of concrete aids and manipulatives, problem-solving and group work.

In Maths — No Problem! Primary 2, these features are exemplified throughout the chapters:

Chapter Opener

Familiar events or occurrences that serve as an introduction for pupils.

In Focus

Includes questions related to various lesson objectives as an introductory activity for pupils.

It is symmetrical.

line of symmetry

Let's Learn

Introduces new concepts through a C-P-A approach with the use of engaging pictures and manipulatives. Guided examples are provided for reinforcement.

Activity Time

Provides pupils with opportunities to work as individuals or in small groups to explore mathematical concepts or to play games.

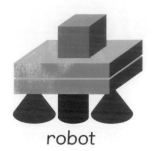

robot

Guided Practice

Comprises questions for further consolidation and for the immediate evaluation of pupils' learning.

Mind Workout

Challenging non-routine questions for pupils to apply relevant heuristics and to develop higher-order thinking skills.

Maths Journal

Provides pupils with opportunities to show their understanding of the mathematical concepts learnt.

Self Check

Allows pupils to assess their own learning after each chapter.

I know how to...

☐ draw models for different situations.
☐ solve word problems.

Self Check

Contents

Chapter 11

Two-Dimensional Shapes

Chapter 12

Three-Dimensional Shapes

Chapter 13	Fractions	Page

89 marbles

How many marbles does Amira have left?
How do we find out?

Chapter 9
More Word Problems

Solving Word Problems

In Focus

How do we find the number of marbles Amira has left? Should we add or subtract?

I had 89 marbles. I gave 16 marbles to Sam and 9 marbles to Emma.

Let's Learn

1. Amira had 89 marbles.
   She gave 16 marbles to Sam and 9 marbles to Emma.

   (a) How many marbles did Amira give away altogether?

   (b) How many marbles did Amira have left?

   (a) 16 + 9 = 25
   Amira gave away 25 marbles altogether.

   (b) 89 − 25 = 64
   Amira had 64 marbles left.

We add to find the number of marbles Amira gave away.

We subtract to find the number of marbles Amira had left.

2 Emma had 42 stickers and Amira had 81 stickers.
Then, Emma bought 20 more stickers.

(a) How many stickers did Emma have after buying 20 more stickers?

(b) How many more stickers than Emma did Amira have after Emma bought more?

(a)

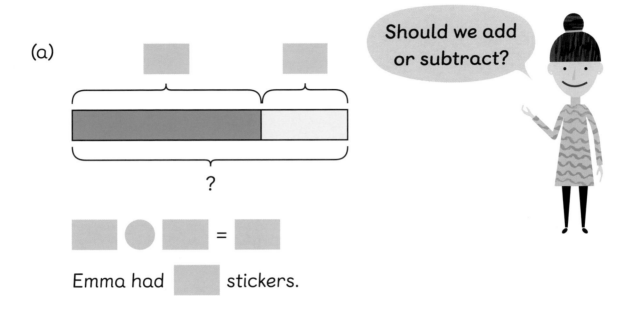

Emma had ▢ stickers.

(b)

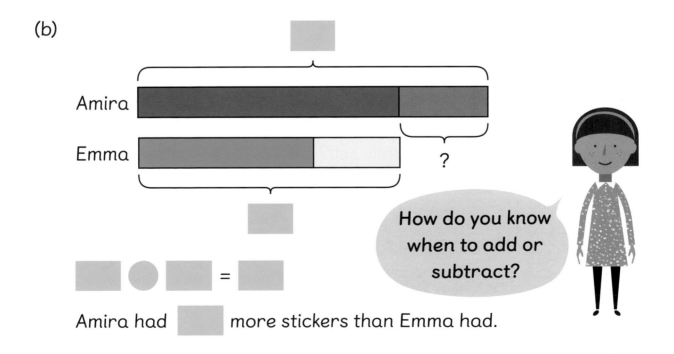

Amira had ▢ more stickers than Emma had.

Solve.

1 Ruby baked 50 strawberry tarts and 50 cherry tarts.
She gave 67 tarts away.

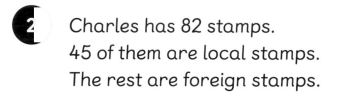

(a)   How many tarts did Ruby bake altogether?

(b)   How many tarts did she have left?

2 Charles has 82 stamps.
45 of them are local stamps.
The rest are foreign stamps.

(a)   How many foreign stamps does
Charles have?

(b)   How many more local stamps than
foreign stamps does Charles have?

3 Ravi sold 42 books.
He sold 29 fewer books than Holly sold.

(a)   How many books did Holly sell?

(b)   How many books did Ravi and Holly sell altogether?

Complete Worksheet 1 – Page 1 - 4

Solving Word Problems

In Focus

The blue ribbon is 31 cm long.
The blue ribbon is 12 cm longer than the red ribbon.
Can we draw models to find out how long the red ribbon is?

Let's Learn

1 is 31 cm long.

 is 12 cm longer than .

(a) How long is the red ribbon?

(b) What is the total length of the two pieces of ribbon?

(a)

31 cm

12 cm

?

31 − 12 = 19
The red ribbon is 19 cm long.

(b)

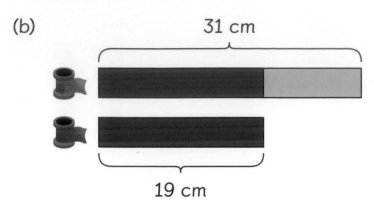

31 cm

19 cm

31 + 19 = 50

The total length of the two pieces of ribbon is 50 cm.

2 Lulu weighs 25 kg. Sam weighs 9 kg more than Lulu.

(a) What is Sam's mass?

(b) What is their total mass?

(a)

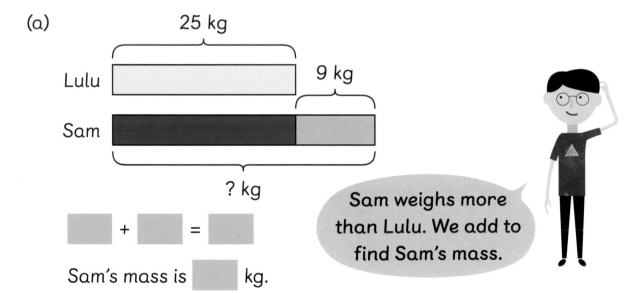

25 kg

Lulu

Sam

9 kg

? kg

[ ] + [ ] = [ ]

Sam's mass is [ ] kg.

Sam weighs more than Lulu. We add to find Sam's mass.

(b)

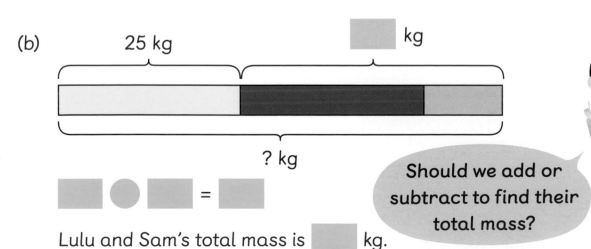

[ ] kg

25 kg

? kg

[ ] ⬤ [ ] = [ ]

Lulu and Sam's total mass is [ ] kg.

Should we add or subtract to find their total mass?

Solve.

1 Amira's luggage weighs 17 kg.
Holly's luggage weighs 15 kg.
Each of them is allowed 20 kg.
(a) What is the total mass of their luggage?
(b) How much more can each girl
pack into their luggage?

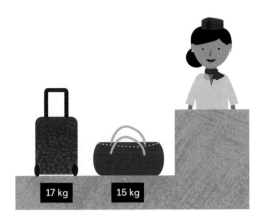

2 There are two routes from Charles' house to his gran's house.

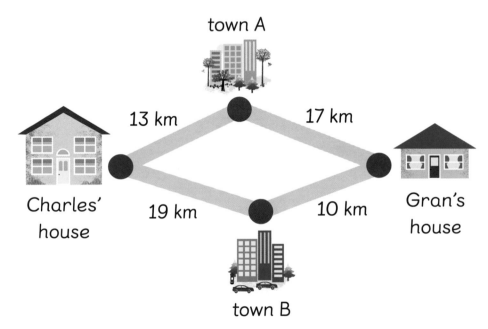

town A

13 km   17 km

Charles'   19 km   10 km   Gran's
house   house

town B

(a) Find the distance of the shorter route.

(b) How much further is the longer route?

3 A bag of flour weighs 13 kg more than a bag of rice.
(a) How heavy is the bag of rice?
(b) How heavy are the bag of rice and
the bag of flour altogether?

Complete Worksheet 2 – Page 5 - 8

Solving Word Problems

In Focus

There were 46 male adults and
49 female adults in a hall.
There were 29 fewer children than adults.
How many children were there in the hall?

Let's Learn

1

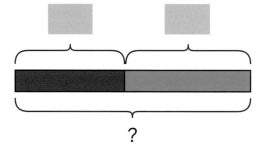

?

■ ⬤ ■ = ■

There were ■ adults in the hall.

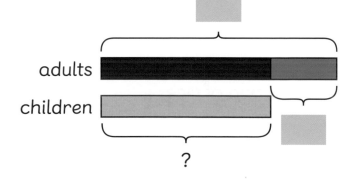

?

■ ⬤ ■ = ■

There were ■ children in the hall.

46 male adults

49 female adults

How many adults were there in the hall?

29 fewer children than adults

2 Hannah baked 38 butter cookies.
She baked 14 fewer chocolate cookies than butter cookies.
How many cookies did Hannah bake altogether?

What should we find first?

 ● ▢ = ▢

Hannah baked ▢ chocolate cookies.

Should we add or subtract to find the total number of cookies?

▢ ● ▢ = ▢

Hannah baked ▢ cookies altogether.

Activity Time

Work in groups of 4.

What you need:

① Make two word problems on addition and subtraction.

② Show your word problems to the class.

③ Get another group to solve each problem and ask them how they did it.

④ Check if they have solved your problems correctly.

Guided Practice

1 35 children visited the library on Monday.
12 fewer children visited the library on Tuesday than on Monday.
How many children visited the library on the two days altogether?

2 There are 51 women in a sports club.
There are 8 more women than men in the club.
How many people are there in the club altogether?

Complete Worksheet 3 – Page 9 - 12

Solving Word Problems

In Focus

 is 8 kg heavier than .

Is it possible to find out how heavy each child is?

Let's Learn

1 (a)

28 kg	20 kg
Is this possible?	

$28 - 20 = 8$
but $28 + 20 = 48$

48 kg is less than 54 kg.

30 kg	22 kg
Is this possible?	

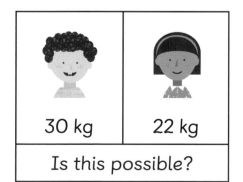

Let's check.

(b)

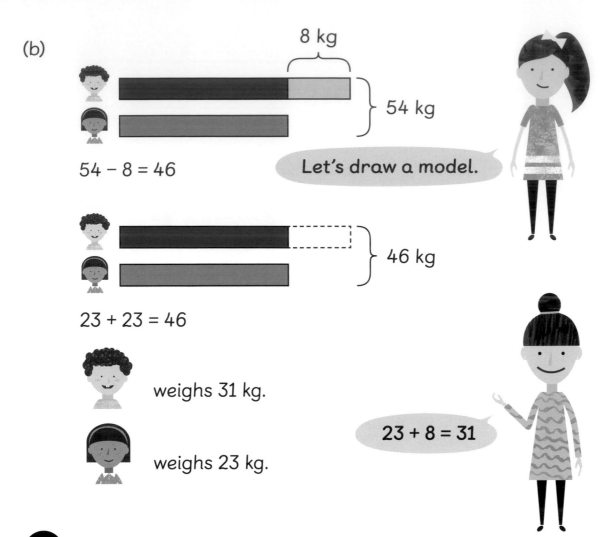

$54 - 8 = 46$

Let's draw a model.

$23 + 23 = 46$

weighs 31 kg.

weighs 23 kg.

$23 + 8 = 31$

2 Lulu had some stickers.
She gave away 25 stickers and bought another 30 stickers.
She had 100 stickers in the end.
How many stickers did Lulu have at first?

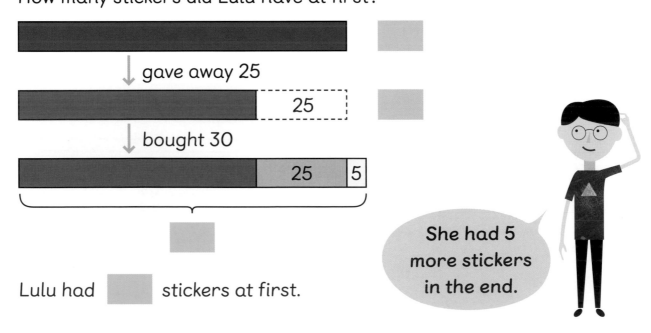

gave away 25

25

bought 30

25 | 5

She had 5
more stickers
in the end.

Lulu had ▢ stickers at first.

Guided Practice

Solve.

1 Charles has 16 fewer £1 coins than £2 coins.

He has 50 £1 and £2 coins altogether.

How many £1 coins does Charles have?

2 A baker took 2 kg of flour from a large bag of flour.
He bought a small 8 kg bag of flour and added it
into the large bag of flour.
As a result, the large bag had 21 kg of flour.
What was the mass of the large bag of flour at first?

3 Look at the picture below.

What is the mass of ▪ ?

Complete Worksheet 4 – Page 13 - 16

 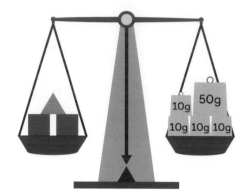

What is the mass of ?

Maths Journal

Look at the sentences below.

> Draw models and answer the questions.

A class has 14 boys.

The number of boys is 5 less than the number of girls.

Write two questions that can be answered using the information given.

Self Check

I know how to...

☐ draw models for different situations.

☐ solve word problems.

How much money does each child have?

Chapter 10
Money

Writing Amounts of Money

In Focus

What does £ mean?
What does p mean?

Show me
a 5p coin.

Show me
a £5 note.

Let's Learn

1

This is a five pound note.
We write it as **£5**.

£ is the symbol
for pound.

p is the symbol
for pence.

2

This is a five pence coin.
We write it as **5p**.

3 Here are some of the coins and notes we use in the United Kingdom.

1p
one pence

2p
two pence

5p
five pence

10p
ten pence

20p
twenty pence

50p
fifty pence

£1
one pound

£2
two pounds

£5
five pounds

£10
ten pounds

£20
twenty pounds

£50
fifty pounds

p stands for **pence**.
£ stands for **pounds**.

Activity Time

Work in pairs.

What you need:

£10

1. Take turns to turn over a card.

2. Show the correct amount of money. Say the amount.

3. The second player checks if this is correct.

This is ten pounds.

£10

4. Take turns to repeat ① to ③.

Guided Practice

1 Match.

20p •

5p •

50p •

1p •

10p •

2p •

• £2

• 10

• 2

• 5

• 1

• 50

• 20

• £1

2 Match.

£20 •

£50 •

£5 •

£10 •

• £50

• £10

• £2

• £1

• £20

• £5

Complete Worksheet **1** – Page **21**

Counting Money

In Focus

Charles saves  . Lulu saves  .

Who saves more money?

Let's Learn

1 Count on to find the amount.

Charles saves £25.

£10, £20, £25

2

Lulu saves £20.

£10, £15, £20

Both save 3 notes.
Who has more money?

3 Charles and Lulu are trying to show £70.
Who is correct?

Charles

Lulu

Guided Practice

1 Write the amount of money shown.

(a)

(b)

2 Show the amount of money.

(a) £15

(b) £75

Complete Worksheet **2** – Page **22**

Counting Money

In Focus

Sam and Ruby have these coins with them.

Sam

Ruby

How much does each child have?

Let's Learn

20p, 30p, 35p, 40p

1. Count on to find the amount.

Plus £1

Sam has £1 and 40p.

2.

Ruby has £2 and 80p.

Sam has 5 coins.
Ruby has 4 coins.
Who has more money?

3 Sam and Ruby try to show 95p.
Who is correct?

Sam

Ruby

Guided Practice

1 Write the amount of money shown.

(a)

(b)

2 Show the amount of money.

(a)   25p

(b)   74p

Complete Worksheet **3** – Page **23 – 24**

Counting Money

In Focus

Ravi is trying to pay seven pounds and seventy-five pence.

£7 and 75p

Does he have the correct amount of money?

Let's Learn

1 Count the pounds.

£5, £7

Count the pence.

20p, 40p, 60p, 65p

The total amount is £7 and 65p.

He does not have the correct amount of money.

2 Is this £7 and 75p?

Can you show the correct amount?

Count the pounds.

£5, £6, £7

Count the pence.

The total amount is £7 and 75p.

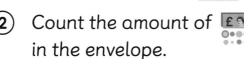

20p, 30p, 40p, 50p, 60p, 70p, 72p, 74p, 75p

Activity Time

Work in groups of 3.

What you need:

① Each pupil takes a ⬜.

② Count the amount of ⬜
in the envelope.
Write the amount of money on each envelope.

③ Put the envelopes in order.
Start with the envelope that holds the most money.

Does the envelope with
the most coins and notes
have the most money?

Guided Practice

1 Write the amount of money shown.

(a)

(b)

2 Show the amount of money.

(a) £10 and 60p

(b) £89 and 25p

(c) £13 and 13p

Complete Worksheet 4 – Page 25 - 26

Showing Equal Amounts of Money

In Focus

I have more money than Ruby.

Sam

I have more money than Sam.

Ruby

Who is correct?

Let's Learn

1

2 pounds

50, 70, 72, 74, 75
75 pence

Sam has £2 and 75p.

2

1, 2
2 pounds

20, 40, 60, 70, 75
75 pence

Ruby also has £2 and 75p.

3 How many different ways can you show 50p?

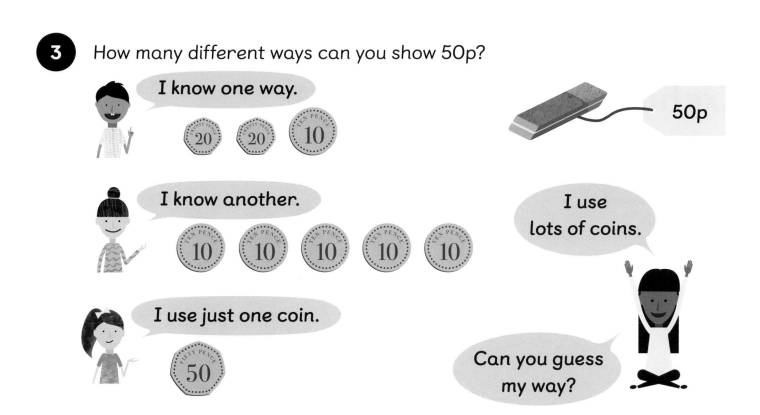

I know one way.

I know another.

I use just one coin.

50p

I use lots of coins.

Can you guess my way?

Guided Practice

1 Use only £2 and £1 to show each of the following.

You can use as many of these coins as you need.

(a) £10

(b) £11

2 Use only 50, 20, 10 and 5 to show each of the following.

You can use as many of these coins as you need.

(a) 40p

(b) 25p

3 Show 72p in three different ways.
You can use any coins.

What can you buy with each amount of money?

Complete Worksheet **5** – Page **27 - 28**

Exchanging Money

In Focus

Emma wants to exchange £1 for small change.

What coins can she get for £1?

Let's Learn

 1

1 one-pound coin = 10 ten-pence coins

Emma can exchange £1 for 10 ten-pence coins.

What is the greatest number of coins she can get for £1?

What is the fewest number of coins she can get for £1?

2 Hannah wants to exchange £2.

1 two-pound coin = 2 one-pound coins

She can exchange £2 for 2 one-pound coins.

Are there other ways Emma and Hannah can exchange their money?

3 We can exchange other coins.

1 two-pence coin	2 =	1 1	2 one-pence coins
1 five-pence coin	5 =	1 1 1 1 1	5 one-pence coins
1 ten-pence coin	10 =	5 5	2 five-pence coins
1 twenty-pence coin	20 =	10 10	2 ten-pence coins
1 fifty-pence coin	50 =	10 10 10 10 10	5 ten-pence coins

Use play money to show other ways to exchange.

Guided Practice

1 Use coins to show the same value as each of the following.

(a) 20

(b) £1

2 Find all the ways to show coins that have the same value as 5 .

Complete Worksheet **6** – Page **29 – 30** ▶

Comparing Amounts of Money

In Focus

I have this amount.

I have this amount.

Who has more money?

Let's Learn

1

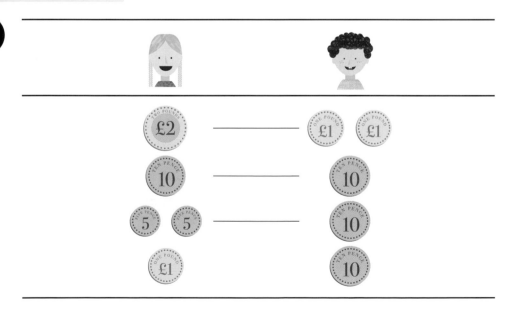

 has more money.

£3 and 25p

£2 and 85p

Which bag of crisps cost more?

_____

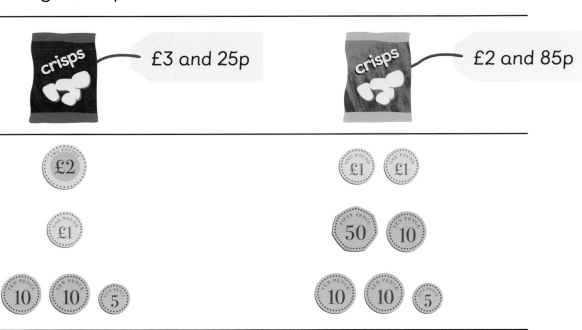

£3 and 25p

£2 and 85p

_____

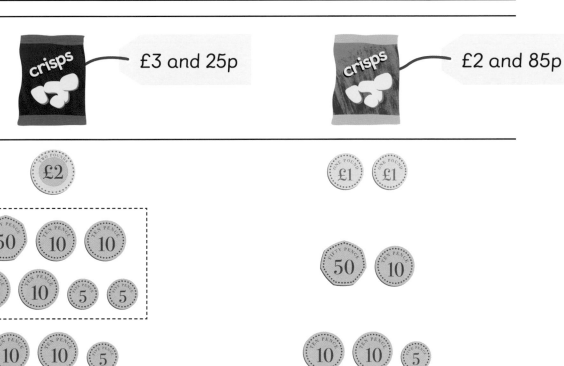

£3 and 25p

£2 and 85p

_____

£1 = 50 10 10 10 10 5 5

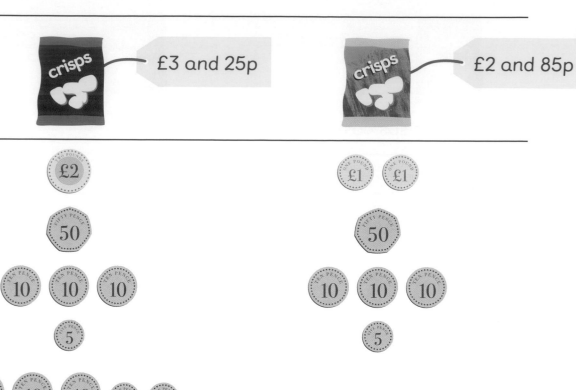

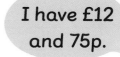 costs more than .

Guided Practice

Compare.

I have £12 and 25p.

Elliott

I have £10 and 95p.

Hannah

I have £12 and 75p.

Ruby

(a)   Who has more money, Elliott or Hannah?

(b)   Who has more money, Hannah or Ruby?

(c)   Who has less money, Elliott or Ruby?

(d)   Arrange the amounts of money in order.
      Start with the smallest amount.

        ,   ,

Complete Worksheet 7 – Page 31 – 32

Calculating Total Amount

In Focus

What is the total cost of the sandwich and the toy?

Let's Learn

1 Sam buys a sandwich for £3.
He also buys a toy for £9.
How much does Sam pay in all?

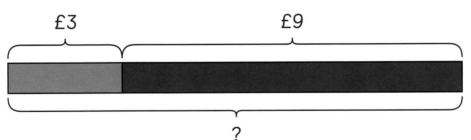

£3 + £9 = £12
Sam pays £12 in all.

How can we check our answer?

£12 − £9 = £3
£12 − £3 = £9
Our answer is right!

2 Hannah saves 40p on Monday.
She saves 15p on Tuesday.
She saves 30p on Wednesday.

(a) How much in total does Hannah save on Monday and Tuesday?

(b) How much in total does Hannah save on the three days?

(a)

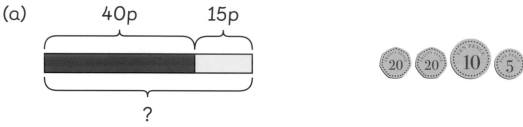

40p + 15p = 55p

Hannah saves ⬜ on Monday and Tuesday.

(b)

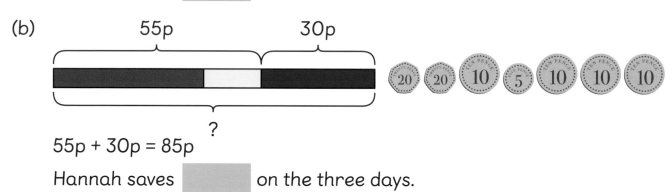

55p + 30p = 85p

Hannah saves ⬜ on the three days.

Guided Practice

How much do these cost altogether?

(a)

45p   39p   ⬜

(b)

£2   £2   45p   ⬜

45p

Complete Worksheet **8** – Page **33 – 34**

Calculating Change

In Focus

Charles had £100.
He bought a cake which cost £25.
He bought a pair of shoes which cost £65.
How much money did he have left?

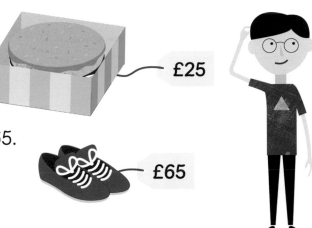

Let's Learn

1

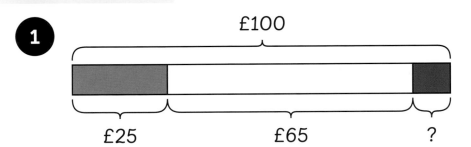

£100

£25   £65   ?

£25 + £65 = £90

Charles spent ▢ altogether.

£100 − £90 = £10

Charles had ▢ left.

First, we should find how much money Charles spent altogether.

2 Emma buys a calculator for £8.
She buys a dictionary for £9.
She gives the cashier £50.
How much change does Emma get?

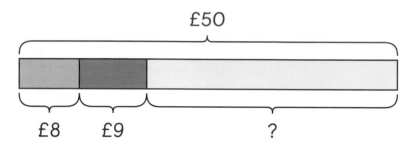

£50

£8   £9   ?

□ ● □ = □

Emma spends □ in all.

□ ● □ = □

Emma gets □ change.

What should we find first?

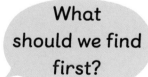

Solve the problem in another way.

'Change' is the amount of money Emma gets back.

Work in groups of 4.

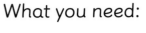

(1) Choose one pupil to be the shopkeeper.

(2) Look at the things.

supermarket

easel

£17

building bricks

£29

sports shoes

£48

teddy bear

£13

train set

£35

(3) Choose two things.

(4) Use 🖼 to show the cost of each thing.

(5) Add and tell how much the two things cost altogether.

(6) Use £100 or £50 to pay for the things.
Get change from the shopkeeper.

(7) Ask your classmates to check your answers.

(8) Repeat (1) to (7).

Guided Practice

Solve.

1 Sam bought a bar of chocolate for £4.
He also bought a bottle of milk for £2.
He gave the cashier £10.
How much change did he get?

2 Ravi bought a  and a .

After paying the cashier  ,

Ravi received  change.

What is the price of the 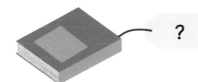 ?

£6

?

Complete Worksheet 9 – Page 35 – 36

Solving Word Problems

In Focus

£17

This costs £9 less than .

How much do and cost altogether?

Let's Learn

£17

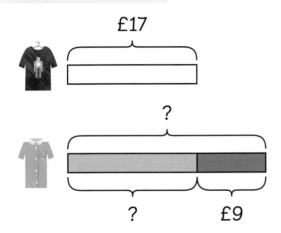

?

?   £9

Method 1   £17 + £9 = £26

 costs £26.

£17 + £26 = £43

 and cost £43 altogether.

Method 2   £17 + £17 + £9 = £43

 and cost £43 altogether.

   £17

   ?   £9

Solve.

1. A snack costs 65p.
   A sweet costs 15p less than the snack.
   How much does the sweet cost?

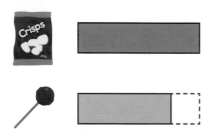

2. A pair of shoes cost £28.
   They cost £7 more than a book.
   (a) How much did the book cost?
   (b) How much did the pair of shoes and the book cost altogether?

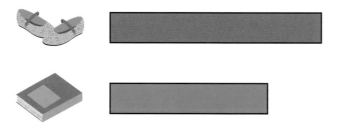

3. Lulu saved £49.
   She saved £3 more than Charles saved.
   How much did Lulu and Charles save altogether?

Complete Worksheet **10** – Page **37 – 38**

Mind Workout

Ruby has these types of coins.

Help Ruby to find the least number of coins she needs to make up each amount.

Example

£4 and 65p

Ruby needs 5 coins to make up £4 and 65p.

(a) Ruby needs ⬜ coins to make up £1 and 20p.

(b) Ruby needs ⬜ coins to make up £3 and 50p.

(c) Ruby needs ⬜ coins to make up £2 and 75p.

Compare answers with your classmates.

We can use to help us.

What should Ruby do?

Our coins and notes do not always look like the above.

Find out what the older series of coins and notes looked like.

Draw your favourite coin or note.

Why is it your favourite?

I know how to...

☐ name coins and notes.

☐ count to tell the amount of money.

☐ show amounts of money in different ways.

☐ exchange coins and notes.

☐ compare amounts of money.

☐ calculate change.

☐ solve word problems on money.

Self Check

How many sides does each shape have?

Chapter 11
Two-Dimensional Shapes

Identifying Sides

In Focus

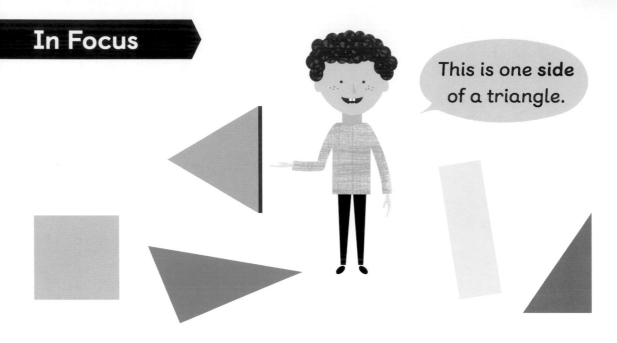

This is one **side** of a triangle.

Elliott puts the 5 shapes into 2 groups.

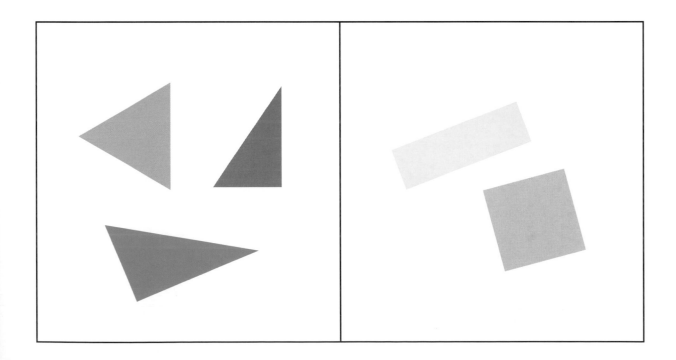

What can you say about the shapes in each group?

Let's Learn

1

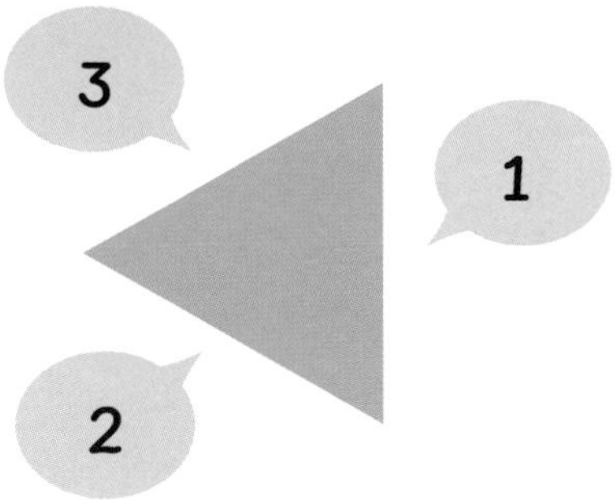

3

1

2

How many sides does ◀ have?

How many sides does ◢ have?

All triangles have **3** sides.

2 This is a square.

has **4** sides.

All squares have **4** sides.

3 This is a rectangle.

has ▢ sides.

All rectangles have **4** sides.

Guided Practice

1 Name the shapes.
How many sides does each shape have?

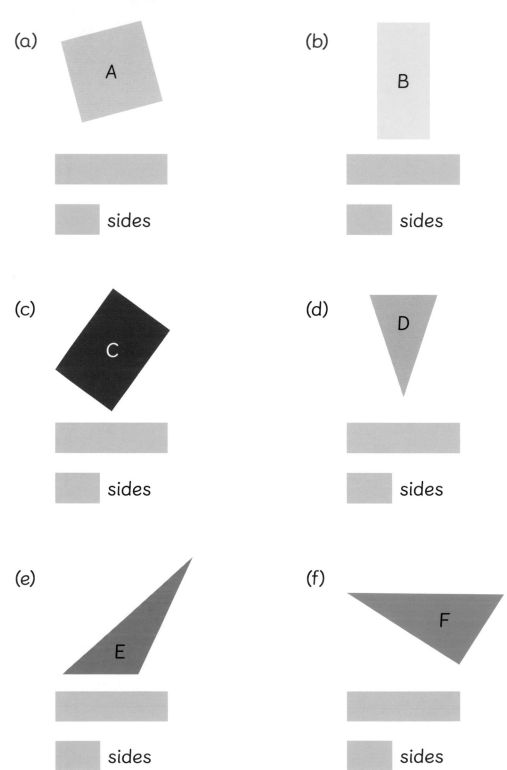

(a)

A

sides

(b)

B

sides

(c)

C

sides

(d)

D

sides

(e)

E

sides

(f)

F

sides

2 How many sides does each shape have?

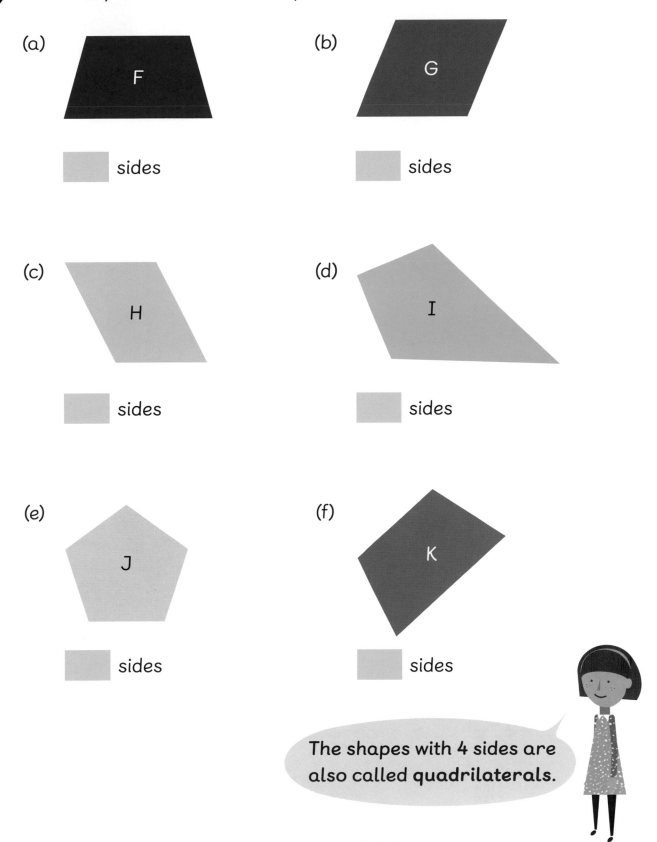

(a)

F

⬜ sides

(b)

G

⬜ sides

(c)

H

⬜ sides

(d)

I

⬜ sides

(e)

J

⬜ sides

(f)

K

⬜ sides

The shapes with 4 sides are also called **quadrilaterals**.

Complete Worksheet 1 – Page 43 – 44

Identifying Vertices

In Focus

These are called polygons.

What can you say about the polygons?

These are not polygons.

Let's Learn

1

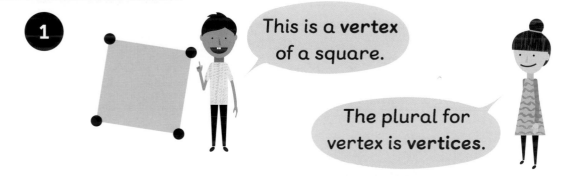

This is a **vertex** of a square.

The plural for vertex is **vertices**.

A square has **4** vertices.

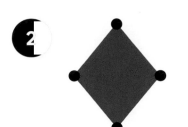

2 This polygon has 4 vertices.
It has 4 sides.

3 This polygon has 3 vertices.
It has 3 sides.

4 How many vertices does each polygon have?
How many sides does each polygon have?

polygon	number of vertices	number of sides

What do you notice?

Guided Practice

1 Name each polygon.
Count the number of vertices and the number of sides.

polygon	name of polygon	number of vertices	number of sides

2 This is a quadrilateral.

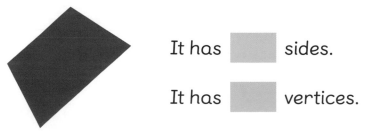

It has [ ] sides.

It has [ ] vertices.

3 How many vertices and sides does each polygon have?

polygon	number of vertices	number of sides

Complete Worksheet **2** – Page **45 – 46**

Identifying Lines of Symmetry

In Focus

Is it possible to find the shapes where one half overlaps the other half exactly?

Which are polygons?

Let's Learn

1

There is another way to do it.

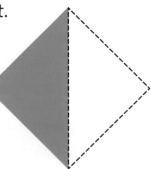

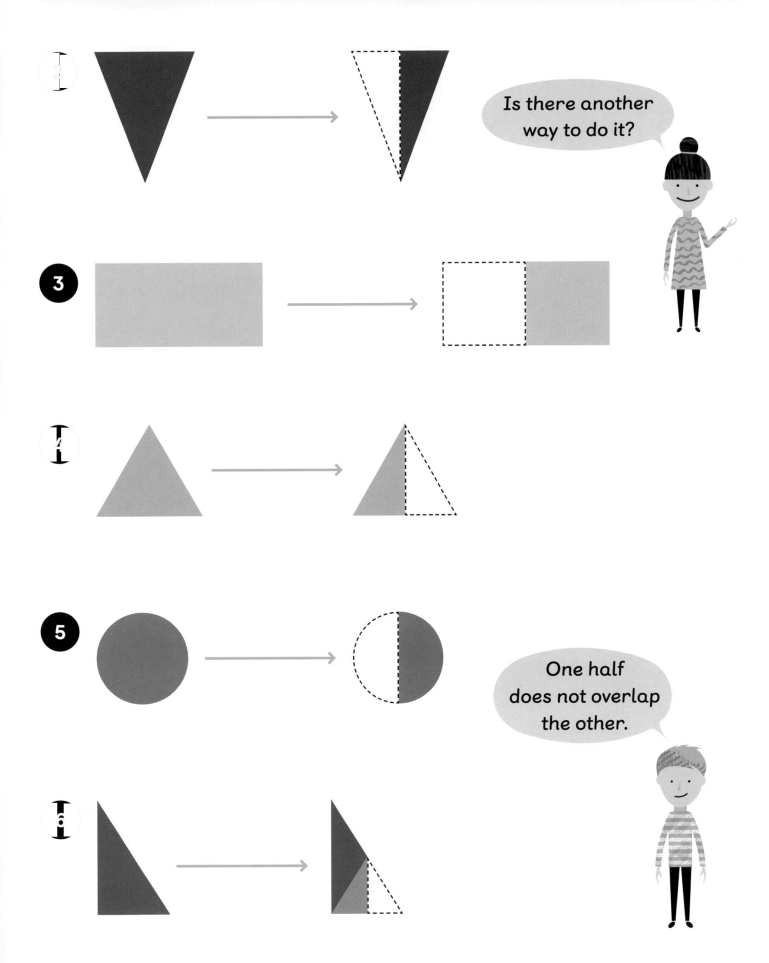

7

This is a line.
We call it a line of symmetry.

We say that a square is **symmetrical**.

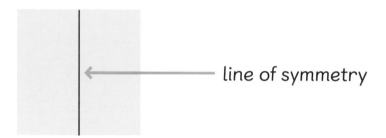

line of symmetry

8 Point at a line of symmetry in each shape.

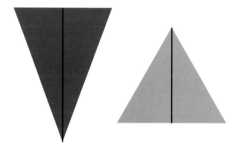

Are these triangles symmetrical?

Is this rectangle
symmetrical?
Why?

A circle is symmetrical.
It has a line of symmetry.

Work in groups of 3.

What you need:

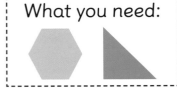

① Try to fold each shape so that one half overlaps the other half exactly.

② Draw a line of symmetry for that shape.

③ Is it possible to find another line of symmetry for the same shapes?

Guided Practice

Answer using **yes** or **no**.

1 Does each polygon have a line of symmetry?

2 Does each shape have a line of symmetry?

Complete Worksheet 3 – Page **47 – 48**

Making Figures

In Focus

Hannah made a figure using pattern blocks.

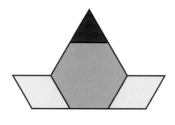

Does the figure have a line of symmetry?
Make other figures that have lines of symmetry using the pattern blocks.

Let's Learn

1 These are polygons.
Do you know their names?

polygon	name	number of sides	number of vertices	Does it have a line of symmetry?

2 Draw 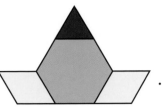 .

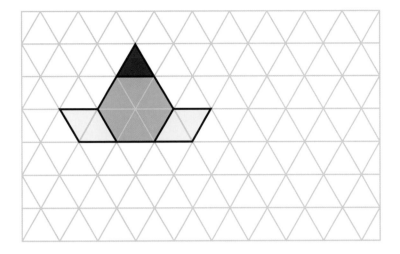

Cut the figure out.
Fold it so that one half overlaps the other half exactly.

The figure has a line of symmetry.

It is symmetrical.

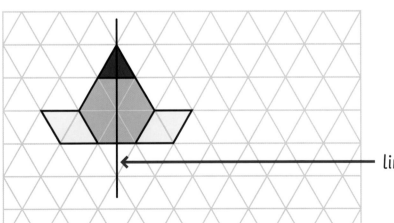

line of symmetry

3 Sam made this.

 What shapes did I use?

 There is a line of symmetry.

4 Lulu made this.

 What shapes did I use?

Are there other lines of symmetry?

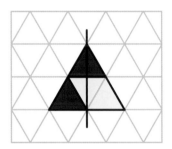

5 Amira made this.

 What shapes did I use?

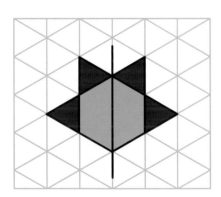

Does it have a line of symmetry?
How can you tell?

1 Which figures have a line of symmetry?

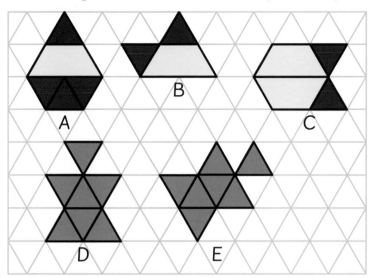

2 Draw a line of symmetry for each figure.

(a)

(b)

(c)

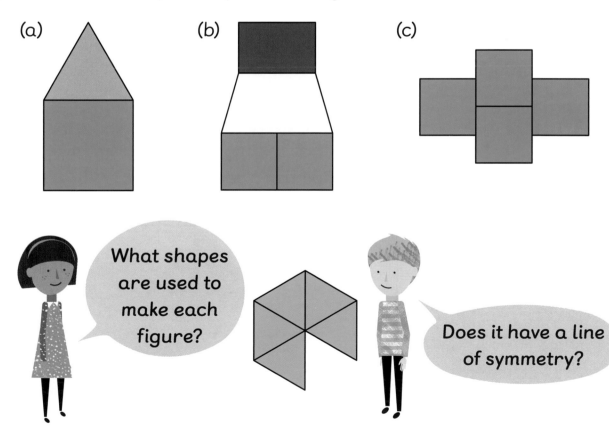

What shapes are used to make each figure?

Does it have a line of symmetry?

Complete Worksheet 4 – Page **49 – 50**

Sorting Shapes

In Focus

Look at these shapes.

Can you name the shapes?

How can you sort them?

Let's Learn

1   Amira sorted the shapes by the number of sides.

3 sides	4 sides	6 sides

2 Ravi sorted the shapes by the number of vertices.

3 vertices	more than 3 vertices

What shapes belong to each group?

3 Emma sorted the shapes in this way.

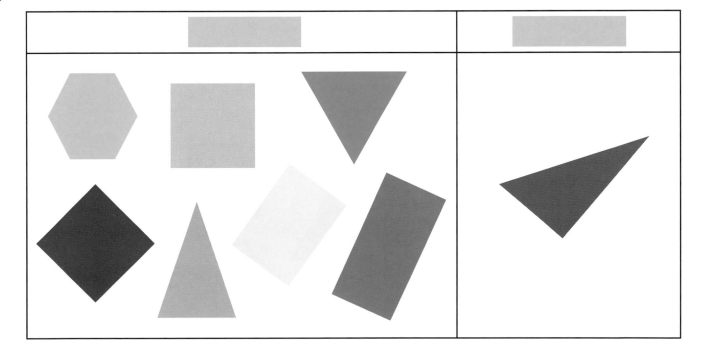

How did she do it?

How are the shapes sorted?

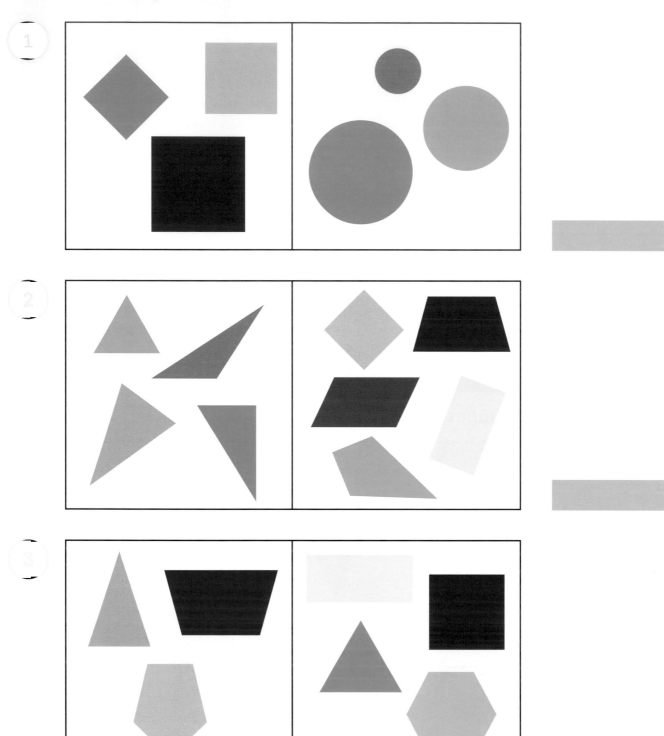

Drawing Shapes

In Focus

square grid

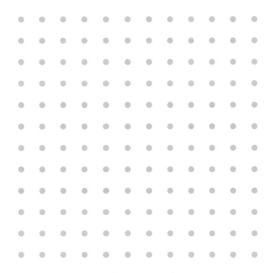

dot grid

What shapes can you draw on these?

Let's Learn

1 Elliott drew a square.

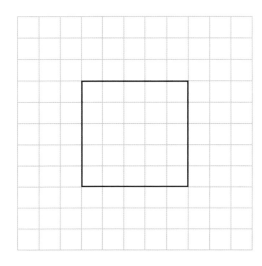

Let's copy it.

Mark out the vertices.

Draw lines to join the vertices.

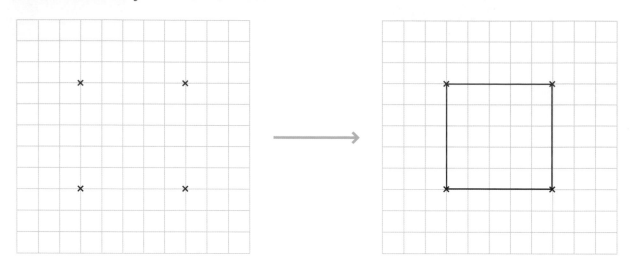

2 Ruby drew a triangle.

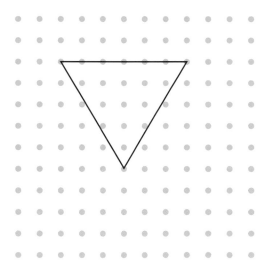

Let's copy it.

Mark out the vertices.
Draw lines to join the vertices.

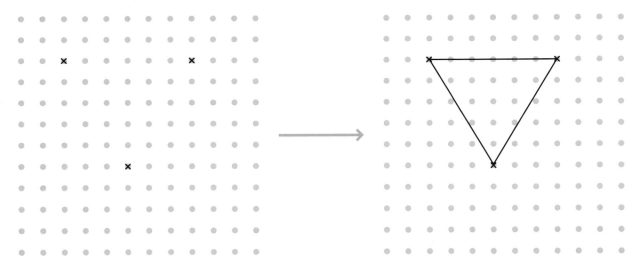

Work in pairs.

What you need:

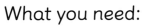

① Your teacher will describe a shape.

② Work together to draw the shape on .

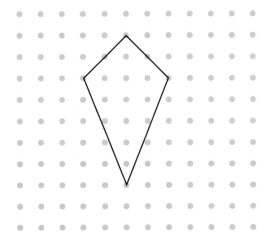

The shape has 4 sides and a line of symmetry.

③ Check if the shape is the one your teacher is describing.

Guided Practice

1 Copy these figures on square grid paper.

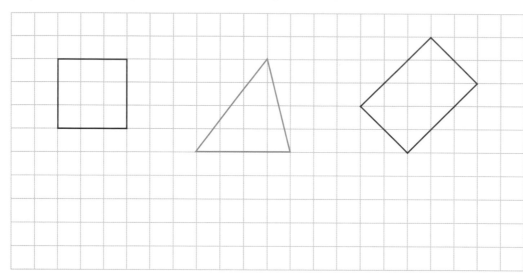

Describe the shapes you have drawn.

2 Copy these figures on dot grid paper.

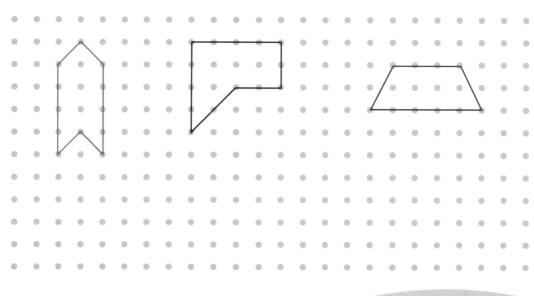

Does each shape have a line of symmetry?

Complete Worksheet **6** – Page **53 – 54**

Making Patterns

In Focus

 ?

What shape comes next in the pattern?

Let's Learn

1 ?

The next shape is ▼.

This is a pattern using different **shapes**.

Look at the next few patterns.
What comes next?

2 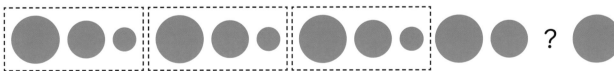 ?

The next shape is 🔵 .

This is a pattern using shapes of different **sizes**.

The next shape is ■ .

This is a pattern using shapes of different **colours**.

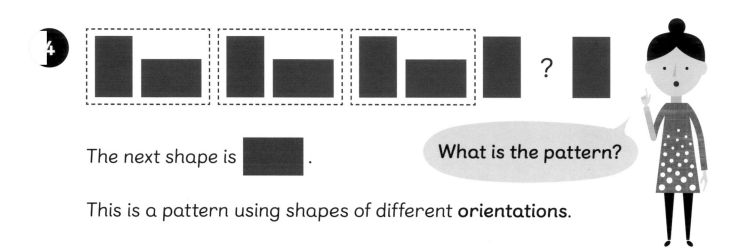

The next shape is ▬ .

What is the pattern?

This is a pattern using shapes of different **orientations**.

What pattern do you see?

This is a pattern using different shapes and sizes.

Work in groups of 3 to 4.

① Think of a pattern.

② Describe the shapes in the pattern.
Ask the other members of your group to name the shapes.

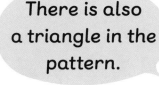
This is a circle.

There is also
a triangle in the
pattern.

I am thinking of a pattern with
two shapes. One shape is a circle.
The other shape has three sides.

③ Trace and colour the  on the to show your
pattern.

④ Talk about the pattern with your group.

⑤ Take turns to repeat ① to ④.

What is the missing shape in each pattern?

(a)

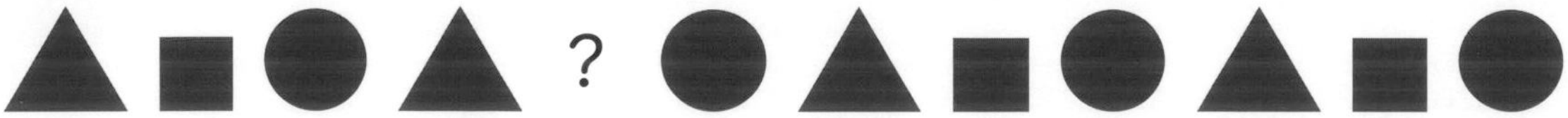

(b)

(c)

(d)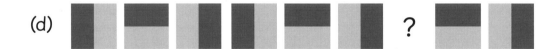

Complete Worksheet 7 – Page 55 – 56

Describing Patterns

In Focus

Do you know the names of these shapes?

Sam used two of these shapes to make a pattern.

1st   2nd   3rd   4th   5th

What is the 5th shape?
How about the 50th shape?

Let's Learn

This is a circle.

This is a semi circle.

This is a quarter circle.

2

The fifth shape is  , a semi circle.
What is the 10th shape?

1st   2nd   3rd   4th   5th

3   The 2nd shape is ⬤ .

The 4th shape is ⬤ .

The 6th shape is ⬤ .

The 8th shape is ⬤ .

The 10th shape is ⬤ .

What do you notice?
What is the 20th shape?

What is the 50th shape?

Activity Time

Work in pairs.

①   Make a pattern using 8 pieces.

②   Ask your partner to guess the 10th piece.

③   Take turns to repeat ① and ② .

What you need:

Guided Practice

1 What is the 12th shape?

(a)

1st

(b)

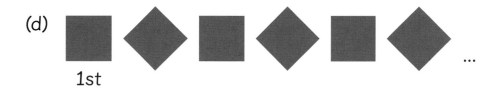

1st

(c)

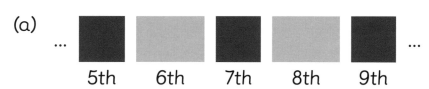

1st

(d)

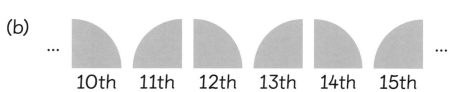

1st

2 What is the first shape?

(a)

... 5th 6th 7th 8th 9th ...

(b)

... 10th 11th 12th 13th 14th 15th ...

Complete Worksheet **8** – Page **57 - 58**

Moving Shapes

In Focus

Amira wants to give instructions to Ravi to move a square piece from ■ to ■ .

What should she say?

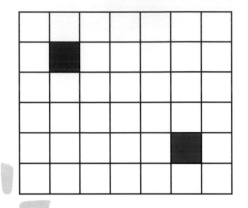

1 step

1 step

Let's Learn

1 Move the square piece 4 steps to the right.

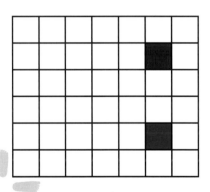

2 Move the square piece 3 steps down.

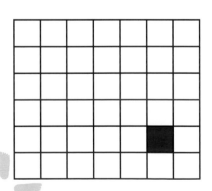

Guided Practice

1   Move each shape 2 steps to the right.

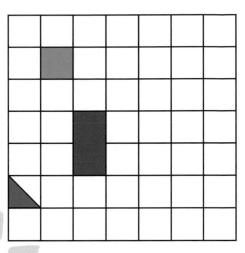

1 step

1 step

2   Move each shape 4 steps down.

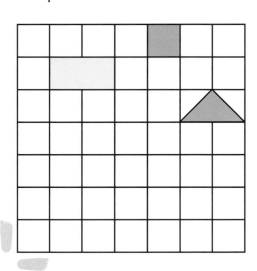

1 step

1 step

3   How can the triangle move to positions A, B and C?

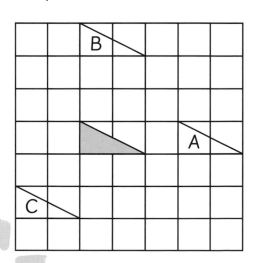

1 step

1 step

Complete Worksheet **9** – Page **59 - 60**

Turning Shapes

In Focus

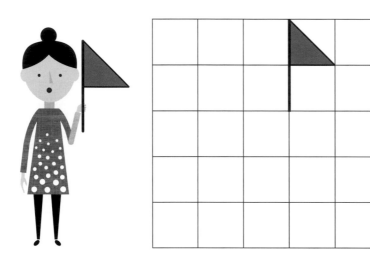

Turn it clockwise by half a turn.

Can you show the flag's new position?

Let's Learn

1. Turn  clockwise by half a turn.

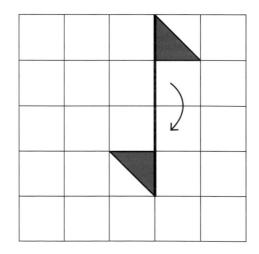

2 Turn 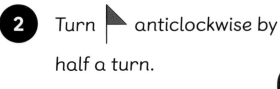 anticlockwise by half a turn.

What do you notice?

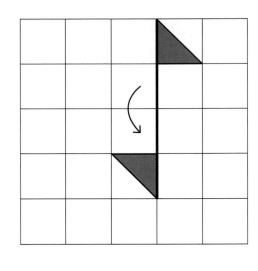

3 Turn 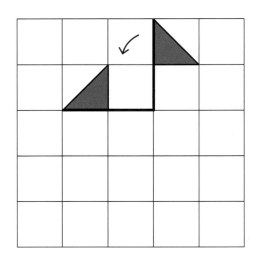 anticlockwise by a quarter turn.

4 Turn clockwise by three-quarters of a turn.

What do you notice?

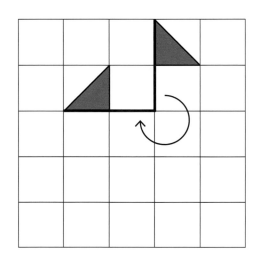

1 (a) Turn  clockwise by

   (i)   a quarter turn
   (ii) half a turn
   (iii) three-quarters of a turn

   (b) Turn  anticlockwise by

   a quarter turn.

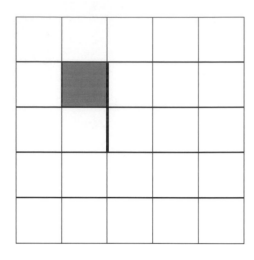

2 Each pattern is made by turning the blue piece.
Describe how the blue piece is turned.

(a)

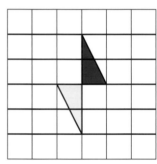

(b)

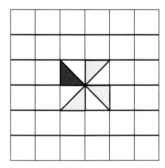

(c)

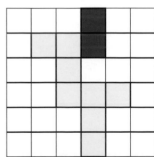

Try it with a cut-out.

Complete Worksheet 10 – Page 61 - 62

Look at the figures below.

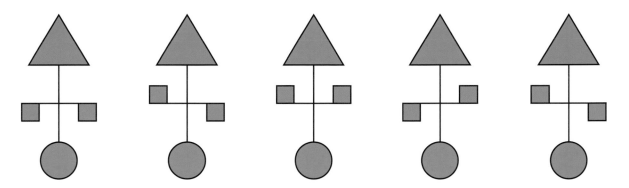

What are used to form each figure?
Circle the two figures that can overlap exactly.

Maths Journal

Write a letter to tell your friend about your favourite shape.

Make a figure using that shape.
You may use the shapes tool on your computer to help you create the figure.

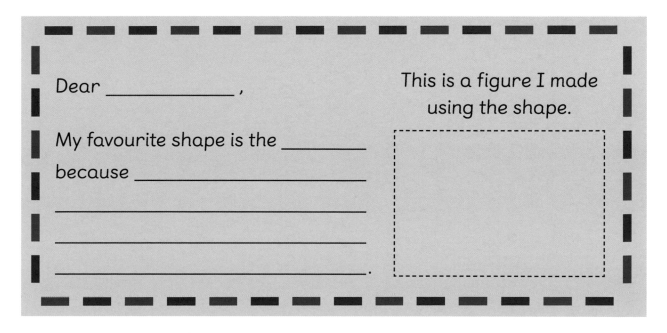

I know how to...

☐ name triangles, quadrilaterals and polygons.

☐ identify the number of sides and vertices of a shape.

☐ identify the lines of symmetry of a shape or figure.

☐ form different figures with shapes.

☐ name the shapes that make up a figure.

☐ sort shapes.

☐ draw figures on a square grid and a dot grid.

☐ make and complete patterns.

☐ tell how patterns are formed from shapes.

☐ move shapes.

☐ turn shapes.

What is the shape of each object?

Chapter 12
Three-Dimensional Shapes

Recognising Three-Dimensional Shapes

In Focus

Move your hand over these things.
Are the surfaces flat or curved?
What shapes can you find in these things?

Let's Learn

1

A ball is shaped like a **sphere**.
The surface of a sphere is **curved**.

A sphere
has no **flat faces**.
It can **roll**.

2

A tissue box is shaped like a **cuboid**.
A cuboid has flat faces.
The flat faces are rectangles.

This thing is shaped like a **cube**.
A cube has flat faces.
The flat faces are squares.

The can of crisps is shaped like a **cylinder**.
A cylinder has flat faces and a curved surface.
The flat faces are circles.

The party hat is shaped like a **cone**.
A cone has a flat face and a curved surface.
The flat face is a circle.

Which of these things can roll?

Work in pairs.

What you need:

1. Put the  in the bag.

2. Cover your eyes with a 👓.
   Pick a solid from the 🎒.

3. Feel the solid and describe it to your partner.
   Guess the shape.

4. Check your answer.

5. Take turns to repeat ② to ④.

6. Look at the solids that you and your partner picked.
   How are they the same?
   How are they different?

Both solids have flat faces.

The cylinder can roll but the cube cannot roll.

Guided Practice

1 Which things have both flat faces and curved surfaces?

2 Match the things with the shapes.

 •

 •

 •

 •

• cube

• cone

• sphere

• cylinder

• cuboid

Complete Worksheet 1 • Page 67 – 69

Describing Three-Dimensional Shapes

In Focus

Touch the edges and vertices.
Look for flat faces.
What shapes are the flat faces?

Let's Learn

1

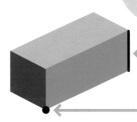

Count the number of edges and vertices a cuboid has.

edge

vertex

The box is shaped like a **cuboid**.
A cuboid has 6 faces.
They are squares and rectangles.

2

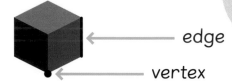

edge

vertex

A cuboid and a cube both have 6 faces. How are they different?

Count the number of edges and vertices a cuboid has.

The toy block is shaped like a **cube**.
A cube has 6 faces.
The faces are squares.

3

 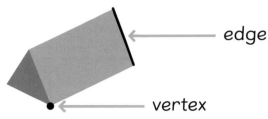

edge

vertex

The tent is shaped like a **prism**.
The prism has 5 faces.
The faces are triangles and rectangles.

How many edges and vertices are there in a prism?

4

 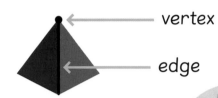

vertex

edge

The toy is shaped like a **pyramid**.
The pyramid has 5 faces.
The faces are triangles and squares.

How many edges and vertices are there in a pyramid?

Guided Practice

1 Match the things with their shapes.

cone	•
cylinder	•
cube	•
cuboid	•
prism	•
pyramid	•

•

•

•

•

•

•

2 Describe each of the following shapes.

	name	number of faces	number of vertices	number of edges
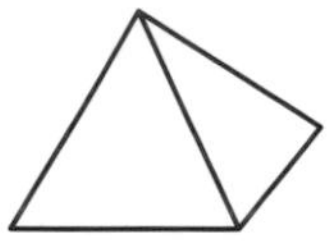				

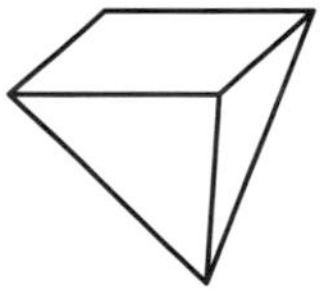				
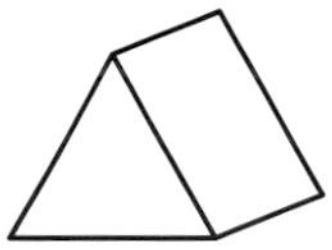				

Complete Worksheet **2** · Page **70 – 72**

Describing Three-Dimensional Shapes

In Focus

Lulu folds some flat shapes into boxes.

After folding, what shapes are the boxes?

Let's Learn

1

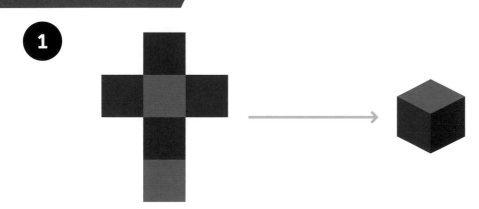

There are 6 faces.
All the faces are squares.

2

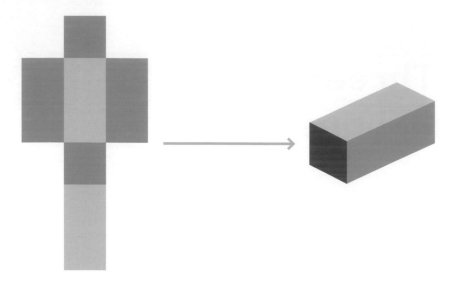

There are 6 faces.

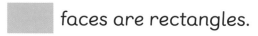 faces are squares. faces are rectangles.

3

There are 4 faces.
What shapes are the faces?

4

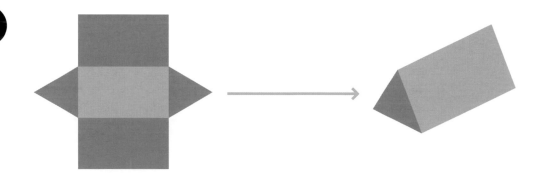

How many faces are there?
Are they all the same shape?

Guided Practice

If possible, name the shapes of the flat faces on each of the following things.

1

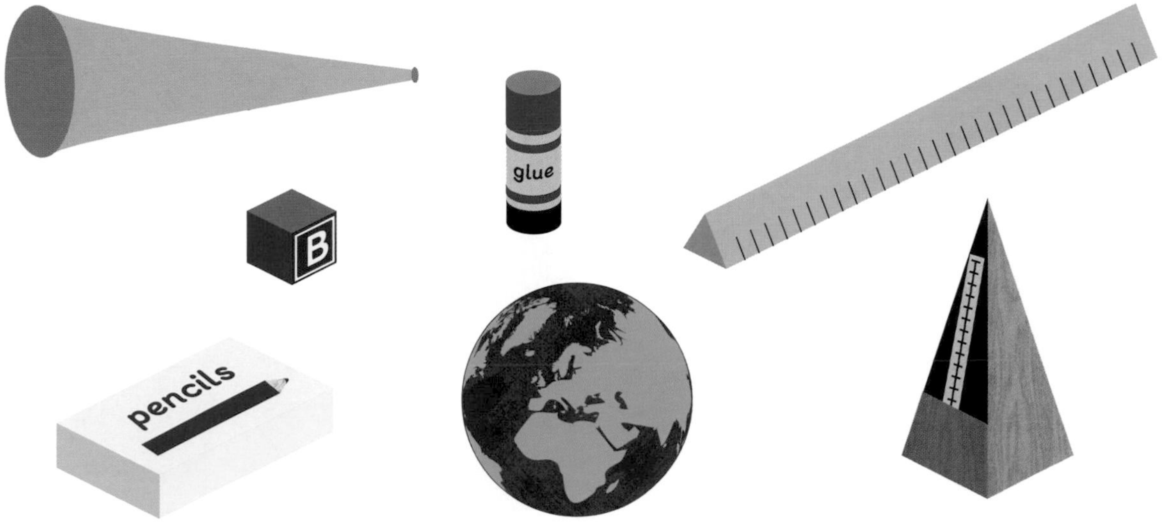

2

Complete Worksheet **3** · Page **73 – 75**

Grouping Three-Dimensional Shapes

In Focus

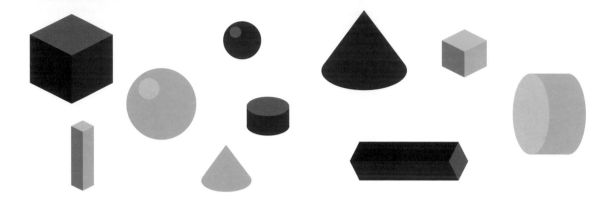

These are three-dimensional shapes.
Match them with real things that can be found around us.
How can we group the shapes?

Let's Learn

1 We can group the solids by shape.

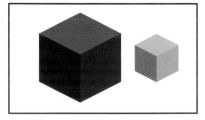

cubes

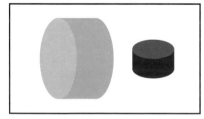

cylinders

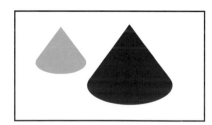

cones

spheres

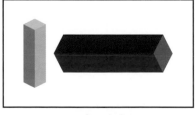

cuboids

2 We can group the solids by the types of faces they have.

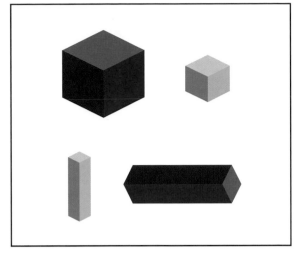

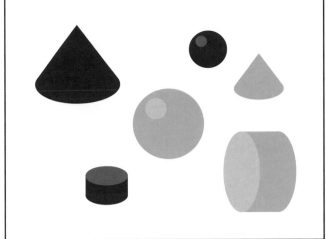

all flat faces

has curved surfaces

3 We can group the solids by size.

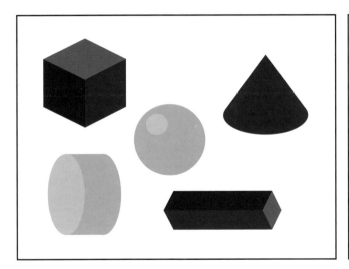

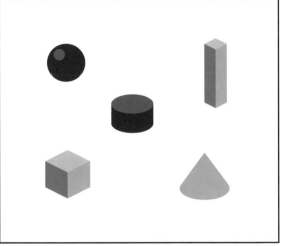

big

small

How else can we group the solids?

Work in groups of 4.

① Look at the  .

Take turns to group them.

② Tell your classmates how you have grouped them.

What you need:

Guided Practice

How are the shapes grouped?

(a)
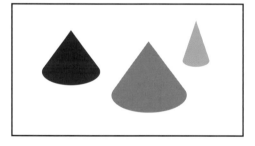

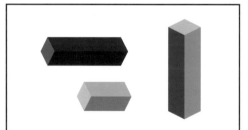

(b)
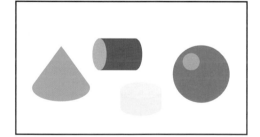

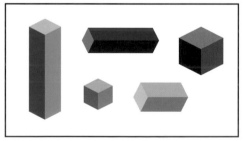

(c)
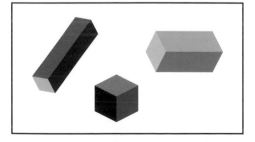

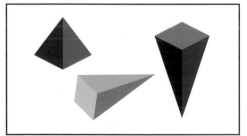

Complete Worksheet 4 · Page 76 – 78

Forming Three-Dimensional Structures

In Focus

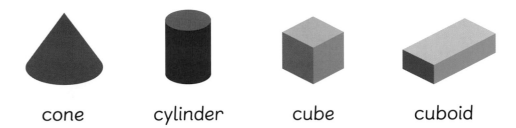

cone   cylinder   cube   cuboid

How can we use the shapes to form different structures?

Let's Learn

Use shapes to form the structures.
Which shapes are used in each structure?

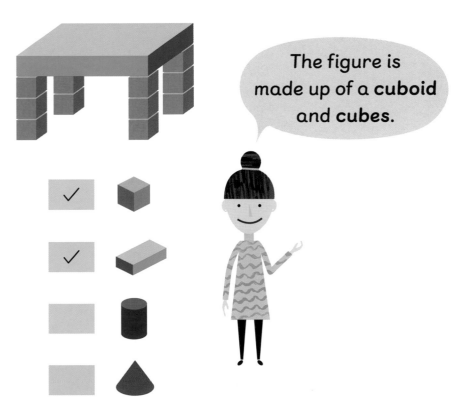

The figure is made up of a **cuboid** and **cubes**.

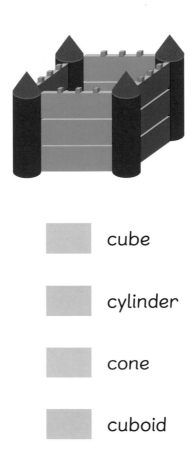

cube

cylinder

cone

cuboid

Work in groups of 4.

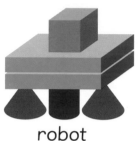

(1) Use the to form two different structures.

(2) Ask your classmates to guess what you have formed.

(3) Get them to tell you which solids you used to form each structure.

robot

Guided Practice

Which shapes are used to form each structure?

(a)

(b)

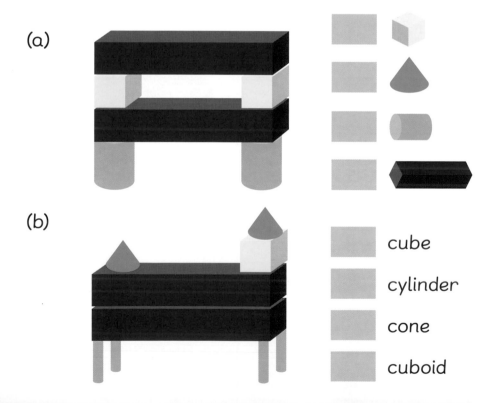

cube

cylinder

cone

cuboid

Complete Worksheet 5 • Page 79 – 80

Making Patterns

In Focus

What is missing in the pattern? How do you know?

Let's Learn

1

 The missing shape is .

The pattern is ⌐cone, cuboid, cube, cylinder¬ .

This is a pattern using different shapes.

What other patterns can you make?

2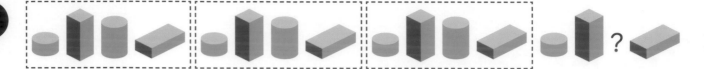

The missing shape is .

The pattern is ┊ small cylinder, tall cuboid, big cylinder, short cuboid ┊ .

This is a pattern using different shapes and sizes.

3 Look at the cylinders.
What is missing?

What pattern
can you see?

Activity Time

Work in groups of 4.

What you need:

① Look at the .
How are they different?

② Make two patterns.

③ Show your patterns to your classmates.

④ Ask your classmates:
What shape is missing from the pattern?
How do you know?

What is the missing shape in each pattern?

(a)

(b)

(c)

Complete Worksheet 6 · Page 81 – 83

Mind Workout

How many small cubes are used to make the bigger cube?

Use ▢ to help you count the number of small cubes used.

Maths Journal

Look at the objects around you.

Can you match the shapes of these objects with any of the ?
Describe the shape of each object.

The juice carton has flat faces and cannot roll.

I know how to...

☐ recognise flat faces and curved surfaces.

☐ name and describe spheres, cuboids, cubes, cylinders, cones, pyramids and prisms.

☐ identify the number of faces, edges and vertices of a shape.

☐ fold two-dimensional shapes into three-dimensional ones.

☐ group shapes in different ways.

☐ form structures with shapes.

☐ make patterns with shapes.

Self Check

How can Amira and Charles share the cake equally?

Chapter 13
Fractions

Making Equal Parts

In Focus

4 children need to share this piece of art paper equally.
How can they do it?

Let's Learn

  The pieces are equal parts.

When you fold it, one piece can overlap each of the other pieces exactly.

Another way is but this is the same way as before.

 Are the pieces equal parts?

When you fold, do the pieces overlap exactly?

3 Are the pieces equal parts?

When you fold, do the pieces overlap exactly?

 4 Are the pieces equal parts?

I need to cut the pieces to show they overlap exactly.

 5 Are the pieces equal parts?

Guided Practice

1 Which are cut into equal parts?

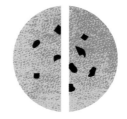

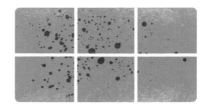

2 Use  .

(a) Show 2 equal parts.

Do it in more than one way.

(b) Show 4 equal parts.

(c) Show 3 equal parts.

Why are the parts equal?

Complete Worksheet **1** – Page **95 – 96**

Showing Half and Quarter

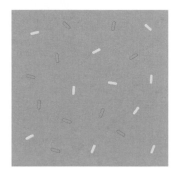

How can Ravi and Hannah share the cake equally?

Let's Learn

1

Cut the cake into 2 equal parts.

Each piece is **half** of the whole cake.
Each piece is 1 part out of 2 equal parts.

We write it as $\frac{1}{2}$.

2 Fold a square piece of paper into 2 equal parts.

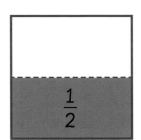

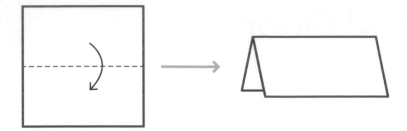
Are there other ways to fold the paper into halves?

Unfold and shade 1 part.

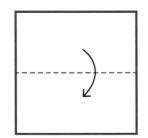

1 part out of 2 equal parts of the square is shaded.

$\frac{1}{2}$ of the square is shaded.

One half of the square is shaded.

3 Fold another square piece of paper into 4 equal parts.

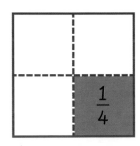 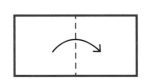

Unfold and shade 1 part.

1 part out of 4 equal parts of the square is shaded.

$\frac{1}{4}$ of the square is shaded.

There are 4 equal parts. The name of each part is a quarter or fourth.

One quarter of the square is shaded.

Are there other ways to fold the paper into quarters?

We also read $\frac{1}{4}$ as one fourth.

Guided Practice

1 Which pictures show $\frac{1}{2}$ of the shape shaded?

 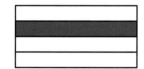 

2 Which pictures show $\frac{1}{4}$ of the shape shaded?

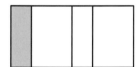 

3 Which pictures show $\frac{1}{2}$ or $\frac{1}{4}$ of the shape shaded?

4 Match the same numbers.

$\frac{1}{2}$ •

$\frac{1}{4}$ •

• | one fourth | •

• | one | •

• | one half | •

• | one quarter | •

• | 1 |

Complete Worksheet **2** – Page **97 – 98**

Showing Quarters

In Focus

There was a whole waffle.

How can we figure out how much of the waffle was eaten?

This is what is left.

We ate the rest.

Let's Learn

1 What fraction of the waffle was eaten?

We read $\frac{3}{4}$ as three quarters or three fourths.

$\frac{3}{4}$ is 3 parts out of 4 equal parts.

There were 4 equal parts.
The name of each part is a quarter or a fourth.
3 parts were eaten.
$\frac{3}{4}$ of the waffle was eaten.

2 Show $\frac{3}{4}$ of a square.

Show by folding and shading.

3 Show $\frac{3}{4}$ of a rectangle.

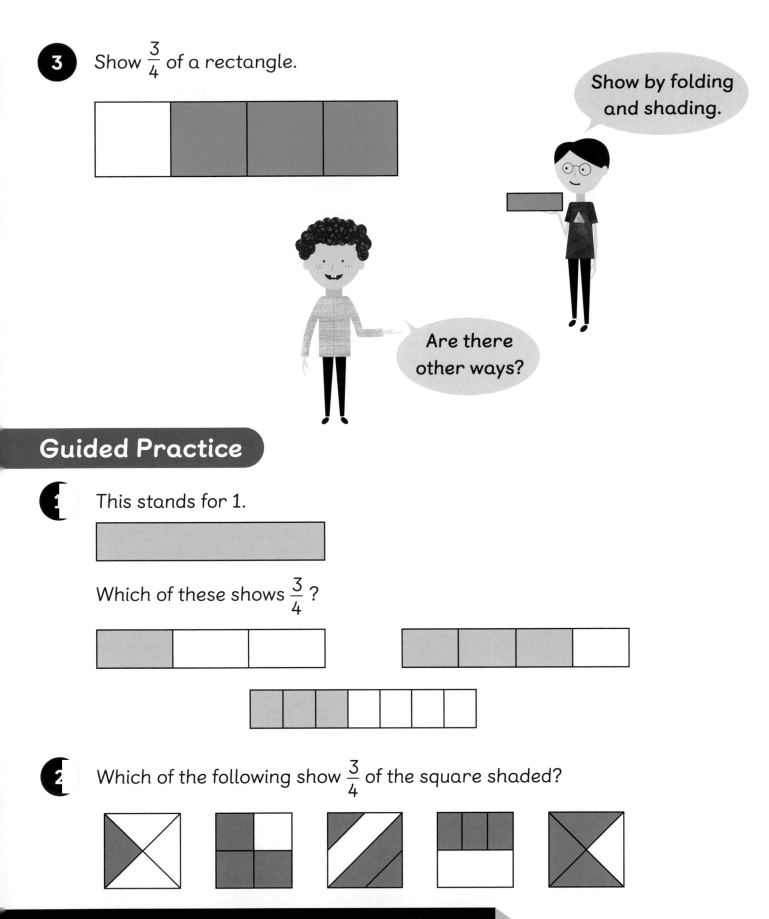

Show by folding and shading.

Are there other ways?

Guided Practice

1 This stands for 1.

Which of these shows $\frac{3}{4}$?

2 Which of the following show $\frac{3}{4}$ of the square shaded?

Complete Worksheet **3** – Page **99 – 100**

Showing Thirds

In Focus

A cake was cut into 3 equal pieces.

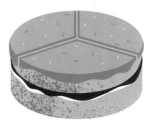

Sam and Holly took a piece each.
How much of the cake did they take altogether?

Let's Learn

 1

There are 3 equal parts.
The name of each part is a **third**.

 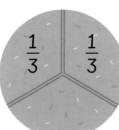 

Sam ate 1 third.
Holly ate 1 third.
Together, they ate 2 thirds.

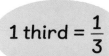 1 third = $\frac{1}{3}$  2 thirds = $\frac{2}{3}$

2

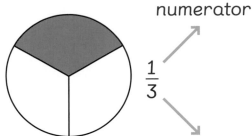

numerator

$\frac{1}{3}$

denominator

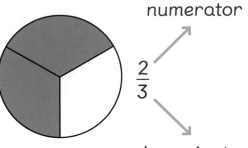

numerator

$\frac{2}{3}$

denominator

The **numerator** tells us the number of pieces.
The **denominator** tells us the size of the pieces.

3

picture	symbol	read
	$\frac{1}{2}$	one half 1 part out of 2 equal parts
	$\frac{1}{3}$	one third 1 part out of 3 equal parts
	$\frac{1}{4}$	one quarter or one fourth 1 part out of 4 equal parts

These are unit fractions.

Guided Practice

1 Which pictures show $\frac{1}{3}$ of the shape shaded?

2 What fraction of the shape is shaded?

3

shows 1.

shows [ ] .

shows [ ] .

shows [ ] .

shows [ ] .

shows [ ] .

Complete Worksheet **4** – Page **101 – 102**

Naming Fractions

In Focus

Ravi

This whole thing is 1.

Ruby

I think the shaded part is half.

Is Ruby correct?

Let's Learn

1

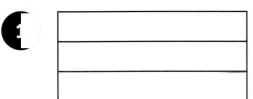

3 equal parts make 1.
The name of each part is a **third**.
The denominator is 3.

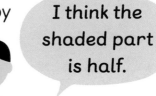
$$\frac{}{3}$$

2 Show half.

2 equal parts make 1.
The name of each part is a **half**.
The denominator is 2.

$$\frac{}{2}$$

3 What if 4 equal parts make 1?

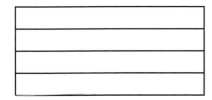

The name of each part
is a quarter or a fourth.
The denominator is 4.

$$\frac{}{4}$$

4

1

$\frac{1}{2}$	$\frac{1}{2}$

$\frac{1}{3}$	$\frac{1}{3}$	$\frac{1}{3}$

$\frac{1}{4}$	$\frac{1}{4}$	$\frac{1}{4}$	$\frac{1}{4}$

5

The numerator is 1.

This is 1 half.

The numerator is 2.

These are 2 halves.

6

The numerator is 1.

This is 1 third.

The numerator is 2.

These are 2 thirds.

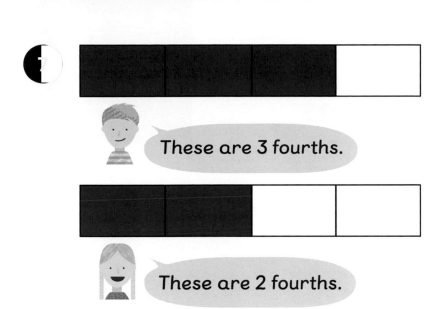

These are 3 fourths.

The numerator is ☐ .

These are 2 fourths.

The numerator is ☐ .

Guided Practice

1 Match and fill in the blanks.

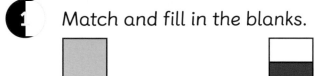

1          $\frac{1}{2}$ $\frac{2}{3}$ $\frac{2}{4}$

numerator = ☐   numerator = ☐   numerator = ☐

denominator = ☐   denominator = ☐   denominator = ☐

2 What fraction of the circle is shaded?

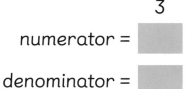

The name of each part is a ☐ .

denominator = ☐

The name of each part is a ☐ .

denominator = ☐

Complete Worksheet 5 – Page **103 - 104**

Making Equal Fractions

In Focus

Charles and Ruby order 2 pizzas
of the same size.
Ruby eats 3 equal pieces of her pizza.
Charles eats 4 equal pieces of his pizza.
They eat the same amount of pizza.
Is this possible?

Charles   Ruby

Let's Learn

The pizza is divided
into 3 equal parts.

3 thirds make 1 whole.

Each part
is 1 third.

The pizza is divided
into 4 equal parts.

4 quarters or
4 fourths make 1 whole.

Each part
is 1 quarter or
1 fourth.

2 The circle is divided into 2 equal parts.

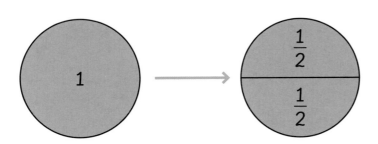

1 → $\frac{1}{2}$ $\frac{1}{2}$

Each part is 1 half.

[   ] halves make 1 whole.

3

1 whole

$\frac{1}{3}$ $\frac{2}{3}$

Each part is 1 third.

$\frac{1}{3}$ and $\frac{2}{3}$ make 1 whole.

4

| $\frac{1}{2}$ | $\frac{1}{2}$ |

| $\frac{1}{4}$ | $\frac{1}{4}$ | $\frac{1}{4}$ | $\frac{1}{4}$ |

$\frac{1}{4}$ and $\frac{1}{4}$ make $\frac{1}{2}$.

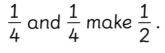 $= \frac{1}{2}$

[ ] and [ ] make 1.
$\frac{}{4}$ $\frac{}{4}$

How many quarters make $\frac{1}{2}$?

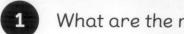

Guided Practice

1 What are the missing fractions?

(a)

$\frac{2}{3}$ and ▢ make 1 whole.

(b)

$\frac{1}{4}$ and ▢ make 1 whole.

2 (a) $\frac{1}{2}$ and ▢ make 1.

(b) $\frac{1}{3}$ and ▢ make 1.

(c) ▢ and $\frac{1}{4}$ make 1.

3
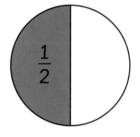 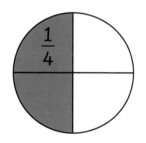

What fraction is equal to $\frac{1}{2}$?

4 Match the fractions to make a whole.

•   •   •   •

•   •   •   •

Complete Worksheet **6** – Page **105 – 106**

Comparing and Ordering Fractions

In Focus

Lulu   Elliott

Lulu and Elliott each has a cake of the same size.
They each cut their cake into 4 equal pieces.
Lulu eats 2 pieces.
Elliott eats 3 pieces.
Who eats more cake?

Let's Learn

 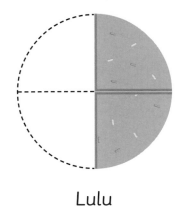 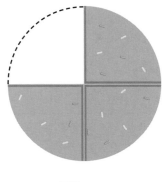

$\frac{2}{4}$

$\frac{3}{4}$

Lulu   Elliott

$\frac{3}{4}$ is more than $\frac{2}{4}$.

Elliott eats more cake than Lulu.

2 Arrange the numbers in order.
Start with the greatest.

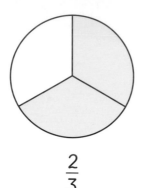

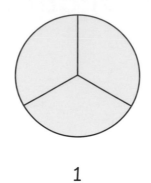

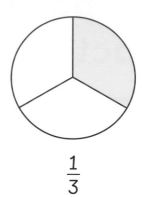

$\frac{2}{3}$

1

$\frac{1}{3}$

1 is the greatest.

$\frac{1}{3}$ is the smallest.

1 , $\frac{2}{3}$, $\frac{1}{3}$

greatest ⟶ smallest

3 Arrange the fractions in order.
Start with the smallest.

$\frac{3}{4}$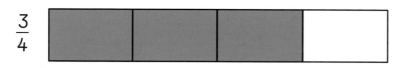

$\frac{1}{4}$

$\frac{2}{4}$

◻ is the smallest.

◻ ,   ◻ ,   ◻

smallest ⟶ greatest

4

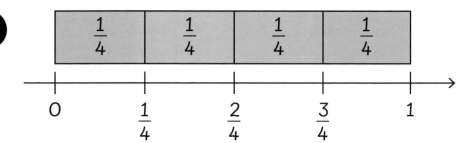

$\frac{3}{4}$ is less than 1.

$\frac{3}{4} < 1$

$\frac{3}{4}$ is more than $\frac{1}{4}$.

$\frac{3}{4} > \frac{1}{4}$

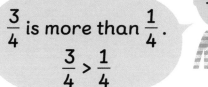

Guided Practice

1 Arrange the fractions in order.
Start with the smallest.

$\frac{2}{3}$

1

$\frac{1}{3}$

☐ , ☐ , ☐

smallest

2

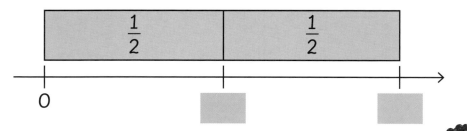

0

$\frac{1}{2}$ is than 0.

$\frac{1}{2}$ is ☐ than 1.

$\frac{1}{2}$ ☐ 0

$\frac{1}{2}$ ☐ 1

Fill in with
> or <.

Complete Worksheet 7 – Page 107 – 108

Comparing and Ordering Fractions

In Focus

Charles and Holly had cakes of the same size.

Charles ate $\frac{1}{2}$ of his cake.

Holly ate $\frac{1}{4}$ of her cake.

Who ate more cake?

Charles   Holly

Let's Learn

1

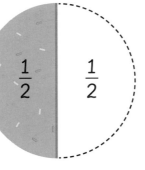

Charles

Holly

$\frac{1}{2}$ is more than $\frac{1}{4}$.

Charles ate more cake than Holly.

What do you notice about the denominator and numerators of the two fractions?

2 Compare $\frac{1}{2}$ and $\frac{1}{3}$.

Which is less?
Which is more?

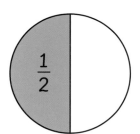 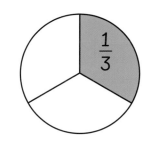

 is less than .

 is more than .

3 Arrange the fractions in order.
Start with the smallest.

Look at the denominators
and numerators in the greatest
and the smallest fractions.
What do you notice?

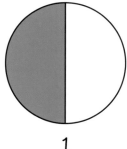 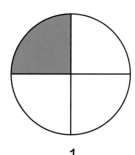 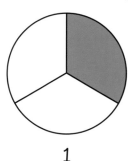

$\frac{1}{2}$ $\frac{1}{4}$ $\frac{1}{3}$

$\frac{1}{2}$ is the greatest.

$\frac{1}{4}$ is the smallest.

$$\frac{1}{4} \text{ ,} \qquad \frac{1}{3} \text{ ,} \qquad \frac{1}{2}$$

smallest   ⟶   greatest

4

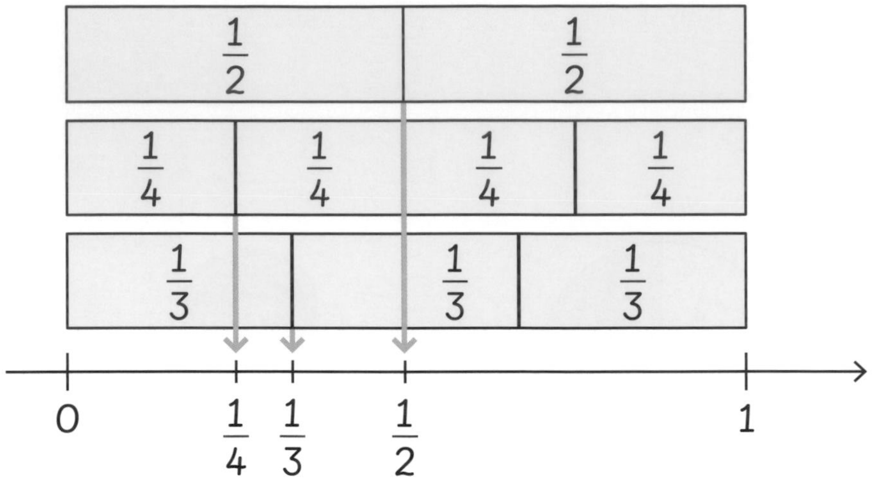

$\frac{1}{2}$ $\frac{1}{2}$
$\frac{1}{4}$ $\frac{1}{4}$ $\frac{1}{4}$ $\frac{1}{4}$
$\frac{1}{3}$ $\frac{1}{3}$ $\frac{1}{3}$
0 $\frac{1}{4}$ $\frac{1}{3}$ $\frac{1}{2}$ 1

(a) $\frac{1}{4}$ ☐ $\frac{1}{3}$ $\frac{1}{4}$ ☐ $\frac{1}{2}$ $\frac{1}{2}$ ☐ $\frac{1}{3}$

use > or <.

(b) Arrange $\frac{1}{2}$, $\frac{1}{4}$ and $\frac{1}{3}$ in order.

Start with the greatest.

☐, ☐, ☐

Activity Time

Play in pairs.

What you need:

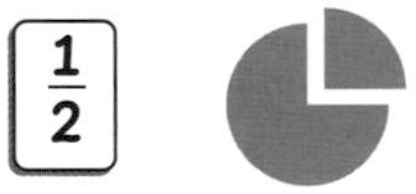

① Turn over all the cards.

② Pick cards showing fractions with the same denominator.

③ Use  to show the fractions. Then, arrange the fractions from the smallest to the greatest.

④ Repeat the activity using fractions with the same numerator.

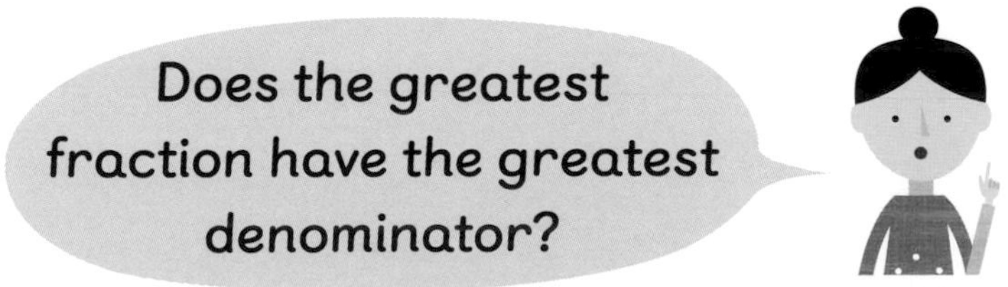

Does the greatest fraction have the greatest denominator?

1 Compare.

(a)

$\dfrac{2}{3}$ $\qquad$ $\dfrac{2}{4}$

 $>$

[ ] is more than [ ] .

(b)

$\dfrac{1}{4}$

$\dfrac{1}{3}$

 $<$

[ ] is less than [ ] .

2 Arrange the fractions in order.
Start with the greatest.

(a)

$\dfrac{2}{3}$ $\qquad$ $\dfrac{2}{2}$ $\qquad$ $\dfrac{2}{4}$

[ ] , [ ] , [ ]

What is $\dfrac{2}{2}$?
It is read as 2 halves.

(b)

$\dfrac{3}{4}$ $\qquad$ $\dfrac{1}{4}$ $\qquad$ $\dfrac{1}{3}$

[ ] , [ ] , [ ]

Complete Worksheet 8 – Page 109 – 110

Counting Wholes and Parts

In Focus

Think about how a group of children can share a length of ribbon equally.

There are in the group.

Let's Learn

1

Each piece is a half.

2 What if there are   ?

Each piece is a third.

3 What if there are  ?

Each piece is a quarter.

4 What if there are

and  ?

 This is 1.

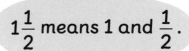

This is $\frac{1}{2}$.

gets $1\frac{1}{2}$ pieces.

$1\frac{1}{2}$ means 1 and $\frac{1}{2}$.

Guided Practice

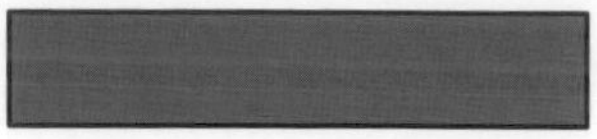 is a piece.

1 How many pieces are there?

(a) 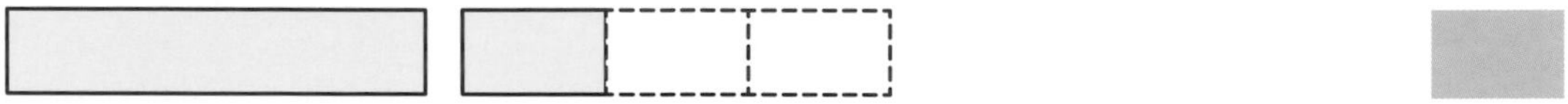

(b) 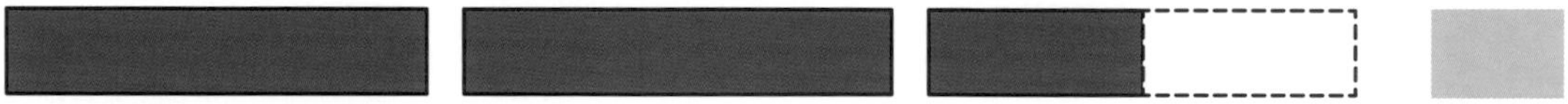

(c) 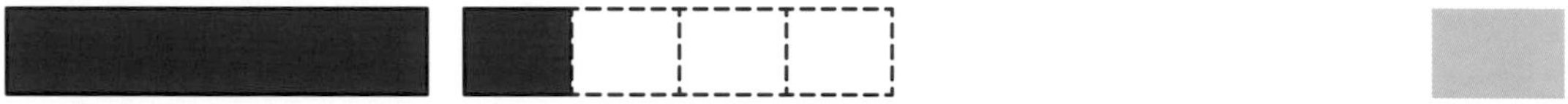

(d) 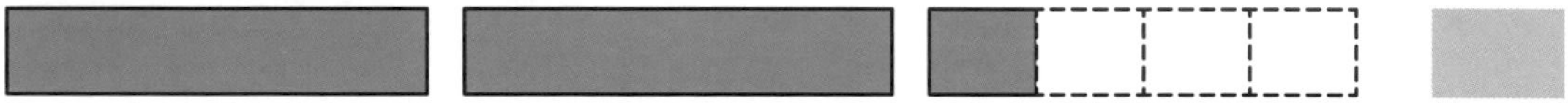

2 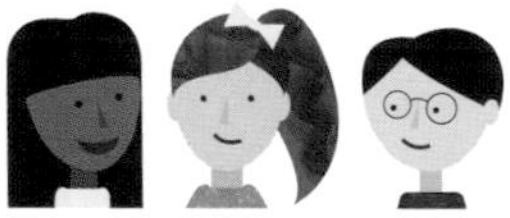 share 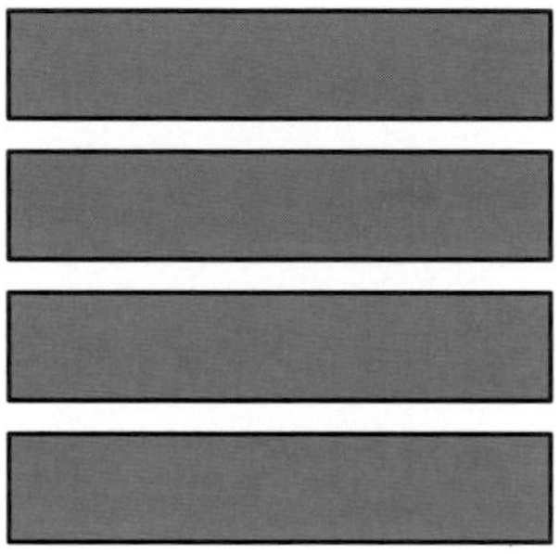 equally.

How many pieces does each person get?

Complete Worksheet **9** – Page **111**

Counting in Halves

In Focus

 Amira buys for an art project.

 Elliott

Amira buys 5 pieces.

She buys less than 5 pieces.

 Hannah

Who is correct?

Let's Learn

1 Elliott

Amira buys 4 long pieces and 1 short piece.

$4\frac{1}{2}$ is 4 and $\frac{1}{2}$.

This is 1.

This is $\frac{1}{2}$.

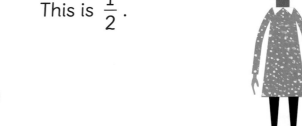

 Hannah

She buys $4\frac{1}{2}$ pieces.

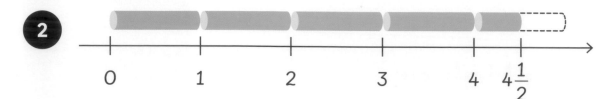

2

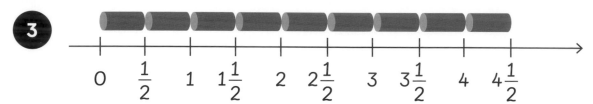

3

 Continue counting in halves to 10.

Guided Practice

1 How many pieces are there?

 (a)

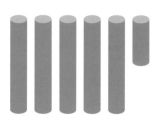 (b)

 (c)

2 Complete the number line.

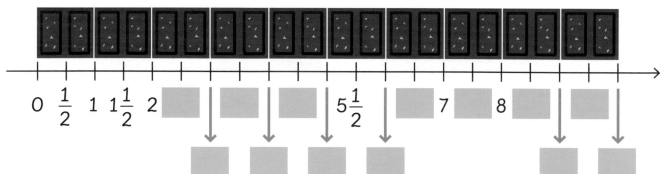

Complete Worksheet **10** – Page **112**

Counting in Quarters

In Focus

How many pies are there?

Let's Learn

 This is $\frac{1}{4}$.

$5\frac{1}{4}$ is 5 and $\frac{1}{4}$.

There are $5\frac{1}{4}$ pies.

 Let's count.

$\frac{4}{4}$ is also 1.

$\frac{1}{4}, \frac{2}{4}, \frac{3}{4}, \frac{4}{4}$.

3 Let's count.

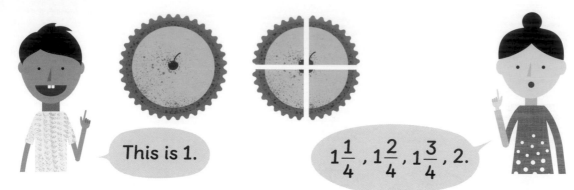

This is 1.

$1\frac{1}{4}$, $1\frac{2}{4}$, $1\frac{3}{4}$, 2.

4 How many pies are there?

3 fourths.

This is 3.

This is $\frac{3}{4}$.

Together, there are $3\frac{3}{4}$ pies.

$3\frac{3}{4}$ is 3 and $\frac{3}{4}$.

5 Count in quarters.

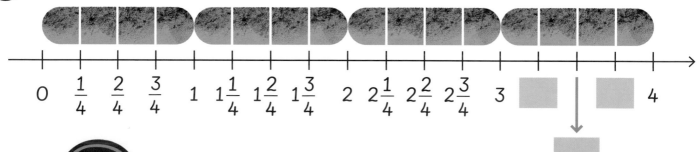

| 0 | $\frac{1}{4}$ | $\frac{2}{4}$ | $\frac{3}{4}$ | 1 | $1\frac{1}{4}$ | $1\frac{2}{4}$ | $1\frac{3}{4}$ | 2 | $2\frac{1}{4}$ | $2\frac{2}{4}$ | $2\frac{3}{4}$ | 3 | | | 4 |

Can you count to 10 in fourths?

1

 This is 1.

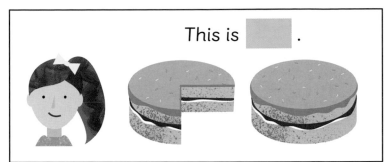 This is ▢ .

 This is ▢ .

2 Complete the number line.

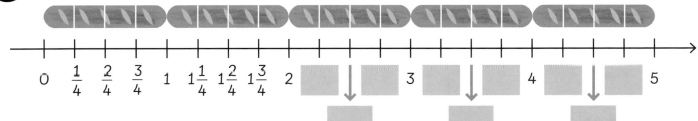

$$0 \quad \frac{1}{4} \quad \frac{2}{4} \quad \frac{3}{4} \quad 1 \quad 1\frac{1}{4} \quad 1\frac{2}{4} \quad 1\frac{3}{4} \quad 2 \quad \qquad 3 \qquad 4 \qquad 5$$

3 Count to 10 in quarters.

$$0, \frac{1}{4}, \frac{2}{4}, \frac{3}{4}, 1, 1\frac{1}{4}, 1\frac{2}{4}, 1\frac{3}{4}, \boxed{}, \boxed{}, \boxed{}$$

Hannah

 4

$$0, \frac{1}{4}, \frac{2}{4}, \frac{3}{4}, 1, 1\frac{1}{4}, 1\frac{1}{2}, 1\frac{3}{4}, \boxed{}, \boxed{}, \boxed{}$$

Elliott

Is Elliott correct?

Complete Worksheet 11 – Page 113 – 114

Counting in Thirds

In Focus

Charles

Emma

Who has more?

Let's Learn

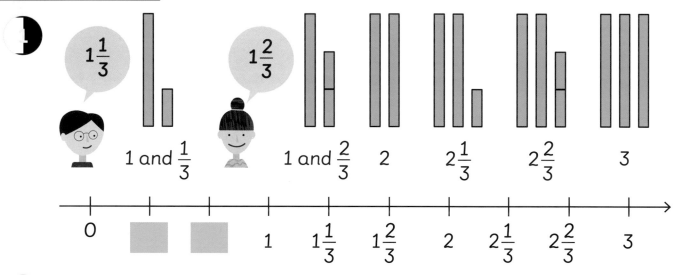

1 and $\frac{1}{3}$ 1 and $\frac{2}{3}$ 2 $2\frac{1}{3}$ $2\frac{2}{3}$ 3

0   1 $1\frac{1}{3}$ $1\frac{2}{3}$ 2 $2\frac{1}{3}$ $2\frac{2}{3}$ 3

Keep on adding $\frac{1}{3}$.

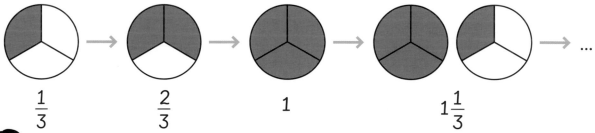

$\frac{1}{3}$ $\frac{2}{3}$ 1 $1\frac{1}{3}$

Count to 10 in thirds.

1 How many pizzas are there?

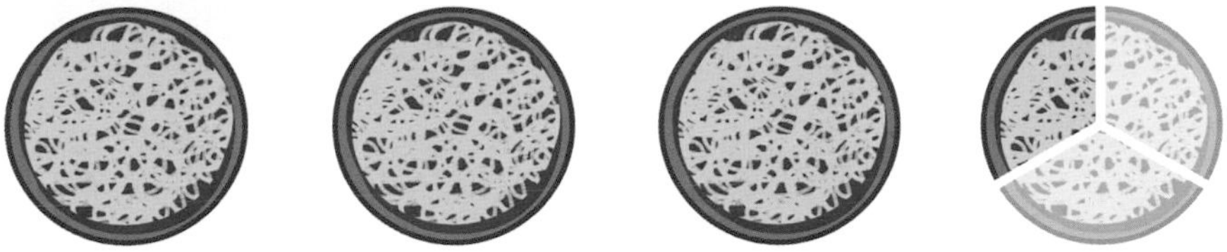

2 (a)

 is 1.

is .

(b)

is 1.

is .

3 What are the missing numbers?

0 ☐ 1 2 ☐ 3 ☐ 4 ☐

4 Complete the number pattern.

1, $1\frac{1}{3}$, $1\frac{2}{3}$, 2, $2\frac{1}{3}$, ☐, 3, ☐, ☐, 4, $4\frac{1}{3}$, $4\frac{2}{3}$, ☐

Complete Worksheet **12** – Page **115 – 116**

Finding Part of a Set

In Focus

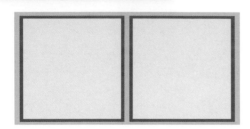

Put the 6 pieces of chocolate equally in the box.
What is half a box?

Let's Learn

 1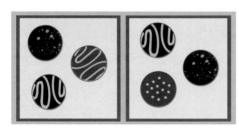

Half a box is 3 pieces of chocolate.

It is like making two groups of 4.

2 What is $\frac{1}{2}$ of 8 sweets?

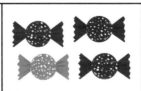

$\frac{1}{2}$ of 8 is 4.

3 What is $\frac{1}{2}$ of 4?

$\frac{1}{2}$ of 4 = 2

Play in pairs.

10

① Pick a number.

② Show the correct number of counters.

③ Find $\frac{1}{2}$ of it.
Is it possible to do this?

What you need:

Guided Practice

1

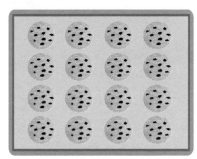

$\frac{1}{2}$ of 16 =

2

$\frac{1}{2}$ of 12 =

3 (a) $\frac{1}{2}$ of 14 =   (b) $\frac{1}{2}$ of 20 =

Complete Worksheet 13 – Page 117 - 118

Finding Part of a Set

In Focus

How can Holly put 6 cherries equally on the cake?

Let's Learn

1 Each piece has the same number of cherries as the others.

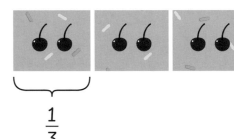

$\frac{1}{3}$

Each piece has 2 cherries.

Each piece is a third.

2 What is $\frac{1}{3}$ of 9 cherries?

$\frac{1}{3}$ of 9 is 3.

3 What is $\frac{1}{3}$ of 12?

$\frac{1}{3}$ of 12 is 4.

| 4 | 4 | 4 |

12

It is like making 3 groups of 4.

Guided Practice

1

$\frac{1}{3}$ of 15 =

2

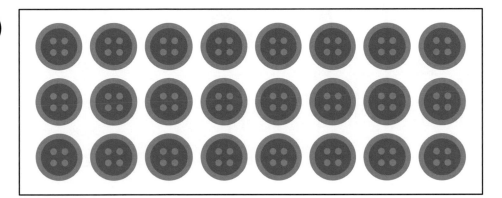

$\frac{1}{3}$ of 24 =

3

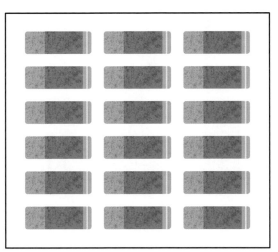

$\frac{1}{3}$ of 18 =

4 (a) $\frac{1}{3}$ of 6 =

(b) $\frac{1}{3}$ of 30 =

Complete Worksheet **14** – Page **119 - 120**

Finding Part of a Set

In Focus

$\frac{1}{4}$ of 20 children are boys.

Is Lulu correct?

Lulu

$\frac{1}{4}$ of 20 is not 4!

Let's Learn

 1

$\frac{1}{4}$

$\frac{1}{4}$ of 20 = 5

Lulu is not correct.

2 What is $\frac{1}{4}$ of 8?

$\frac{1}{4}$ of 8 is 2.

This is a quarter.

It is like making 4 groups of 2.

3 $\frac{1}{4}$ of 20 = 5   20 ÷ 4 = 5

$\frac{1}{4}$ of 8 = 2   8 ÷ 4 = 2

$\frac{1}{4}$ of 12 = ▢

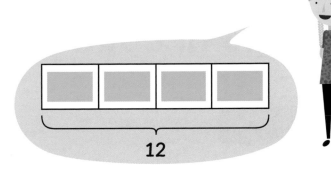

Guided Practice

  1

$\frac{1}{4}$ of 12 = ▢

  2

$\frac{1}{4}$ of 16 = ▢

  3

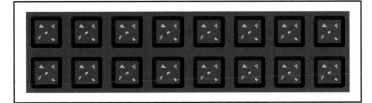

$\frac{1}{4}$ of 24 = ▢

$\frac{3}{4}$ of 24 = ▢

  4   (a) $\frac{1}{4}$ of 20 = ▢

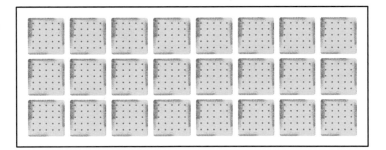

$\frac{3}{4}$ of 20 = ▢

(b) $\frac{1}{4}$ of 40 = ▢

 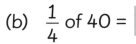 Complete Worksheet **15** – Page **121 - 122**

Finding Part of a Quantity

In Focus

How can we cut a 12-cm piece of coloured paper into halves?

Let's Learn

1 $\frac{1}{2}$ of 12 cm

12 cm

6 cm	6 cm

6 cm + 6 cm = 12 cm

$\frac{1}{2}$ of 12 cm = 6 cm

2 $\frac{1}{3}$ of 12 cm

12 cm

4 cm	4 cm	4 cm

4 cm + 4 cm + 4 cm = ☐ cm

$\frac{1}{3}$ of 12 cm = 4 cm

3 $\frac{1}{4}$ of 12 cm

12 cm

?	?	?	?

$\frac{1}{4}$ of 12 cm = ☐ cm

☐ cm + ☐ cm + ☐ cm + ☐ cm = 12 cm

Guided Practice

1

9 cm

?	?	?

$\frac{1}{3}$ of 9 cm = ▢ cm

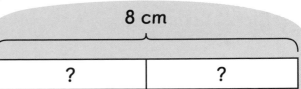

8 cm

?	?

2

8 cm

(a) $\frac{1}{2}$ of 8 cm = ▢ cm

(b) $\frac{1}{4}$ of 8 cm = ▢ cm

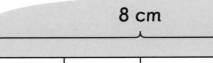

8 cm

?	?	?	?

3 (a) $\frac{1}{2}$ of 10 cm = ▢ cm

▢

(b) $\frac{1}{3}$ of 15 cm = ▢ cm

▢

(c) $\frac{1}{4}$ of 20 cm = ▢ cm

▢

 $\frac{3}{4}$ of 20 cm = ▢ cm

Complete Worksheet 16 – Page 123 - 124

Block A is $\frac{1}{4}$ of a figure.

Which of the following figures did Block A come from?

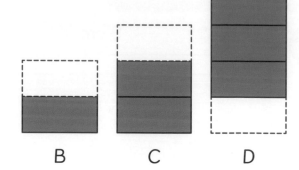

B   C   D

Maths Journal

Find examples of $\frac{1}{2}$, $\frac{1}{3}$ and $\frac{1}{4}$ around you.

Write them in your journal.

Ravi's Journal

   The water filled $\frac{1}{2}$ of the beaker.

I know how to...

Self Check

☐ make and show halves, quarters and thirds.

☐ name and write a fraction.

☐ name fractions that make one whole.

☐ compare and order fractions.

☐ count wholes with halves, quarters and thirds.

☐ find part of a set and a quantity.

Can you help Holly
tell the time on the clock?

Chapter 14
Time

Telling and Writing Time to 5 Minutes

In Focus

What is the time shown?

→ is the minute hand.
→ is the hour hand.

Let's Learn

1

3 o'clock

→ 5 minutes

5 minutes after 3 o'clock is 3:05.

After 5 **minutes**, the minute hand moves from 12 to 1.
We write the time as **3:05**.

Sometimes we say the time is 5 minutes past three.

2

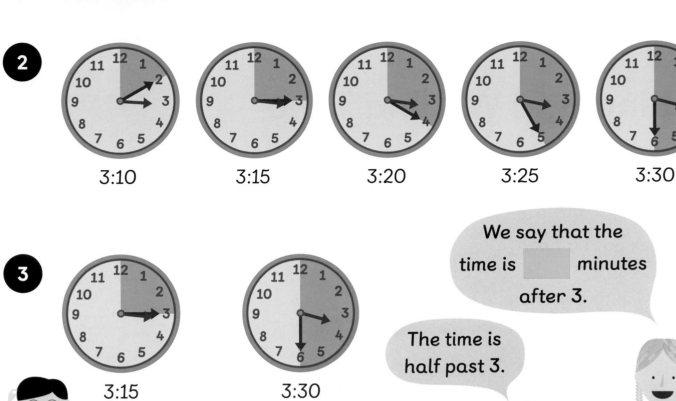

3:10   3:15   3:20   3:25   3:30

3

3:15   3:30

We say that the time is [ ] minutes after 3.

The time is half past 3.

We can also say the time is quarter past 3.

Guided Practice

Tell the time.
Say what you usually do at that time.

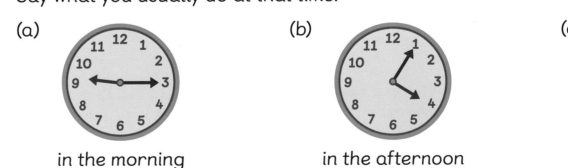

(a) in the morning

(b) in the afternoon

(c) in the evening

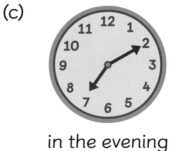

Complete Worksheet **1** – Page **129 – 130**

Telling and Writing Time

In Focus

The clock has stopped.

It is 8:30 in the morning.
Show the correct time.

Let's Learn

1

Where is the hour hand?
Why is it in between 8 and 9 now?

2

35 minutes   30 minutes

After 5 minutes, the minute
hand moves from 6 to 7.
We write the time as 8:35.

We also say the time is
35 minutes past eight.

3

8:40   8:45   8:50   8:55   9:00

4

8:45

Tell the time shown.

We also say the time is quarter to nine.

Activity Time

Work in groups.

What you need:

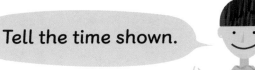

① Each person receives ⬚ 3:15 ⬚.

② Show the time on your

clock .

③ Ask your friends "What time does your clock show?"

④ Complete the table.

name	time

⑤ Show your friends your clock when they ask "What time does your clock show?"

1 Tell the time.
Say what you usually do at that time.

(a)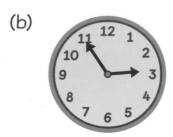

in the morning

(b)

in the afternoon

(c)

in the evening

2 Count in fives to tell the time.

(a)

The time shown is .

It is minutes after o' clock.

(b)

The time shown is .

It is minutes after o' clock.

Complete Worksheet **2** – Page **131 – 132**

Sequencing Events

In Focus

Ruby's diary pages came apart.
Help her arrange them in order.

Let's Learn

1

in the morning   in the evening   in the evening

The time is 8:15.

The time is half past five.

The time is quarter to eight.

2

 Ruby was playing in the park **before** she had dinner.

 She had dinner **after** she played in the park.

1

 Ravi

 Emma

 Sam

(a) Among the three children, who arrived at school first?

At what time?

(b) Which of the three children arrived next?

At what time?

2

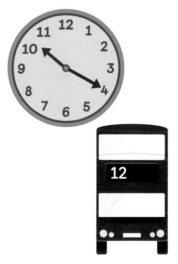

12

7

63

The three buses arrived one after another.

(a) Tell the time that each bus arrived at the bus stop.

(b) Which bus arrived first?

Which one arrived next?

Complete Worksheet **3** – Page **133 – 134**

Drawing Clock Hands

In Focus

Draw the hour hand to show 7:45.

Charles did this.

Charles

Ruby did this.

Ruby

Who is correct?

Let's Learn

1   7:45 is almost 8:00.
    So, the hour hand is closer to 8 than to 7.

Ruby is correct.

2 Show the minute hand to show 4:15.

Count in fives.
5, 10, 15

At 4:15, the minute hand is pointing to 3.
The hour hand is just past 4.

Work in groups of 3 to 4.

What you need:

① Take turns to tell your friends a time when you do your favourite activity.

At 6:15 in the evening, I play football.

② Show the time on the face of the clock.

③ Check if everyone has shown the correct time.

Guided Practice

1 Which is correct?

(a) 8:55 in the morning.

(b) 9:05 at night.

2 Read the time.
Show the missing hour hand.

(a) 10:15

(b) 3:50

3 Read the time.
Show the missing minute hand.

(a) 7:45

(b) 2:20

4 Show the time.

(a)

I eat breakfast at 6:45 in the morning.

(b)

I reach home at 4:15 in the afternoon.

Complete Worksheet 4 – Page **135 – 136**

Finding Durations of Time

In Focus

It is now  .

In 30 minutes, the train will reach Castle Town.
In 1 hour, the train will reach Temple Street.
What time will it be when the train reaches Castle Town?
What about Temple Street?

Let's Learn

 1

Count in fives.
5, 10, 15, 20, 25, 30

After 30 minutes, the minute hand moves from 12 to 6.
The time shown is 30 minutes after 3 o'clock.

The train reaches Castle Town at .

 2

60 minutes is equal to 1 hour.

The minute hand makes a complete round in 60 minutes.
The hour hand moves from 3 to 4.
1 hour after 3 o'clock is 4 o'clock.
The train reaches Temple Street at 4 o'clock.

Guided Practice

1 What time will it be in 30 minutes?
What time will it be in 1 hour?

(a)

(b)

2 What time will it be in 3 hours?

(a)

(b)

Complete Worksheet **5** – Page **137 – 138**

Finding Durations of Time

In Focus

She started to paint.

She finished painting.

How can we tell how long Holly took to paint?

Let's Learn

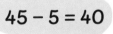 5 + 35 = 40

Method 1

 5 minutes →  35 minutes →

2:05   2:10   2:45

Method 2

 45 minutes →

2:00   2:45

 45 − 5 = 40

↓ 5 minutes

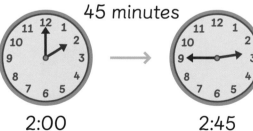

2:05

Holly took 40 minutes.

How long did the kids take for each of the following activities?

(a)

(b)

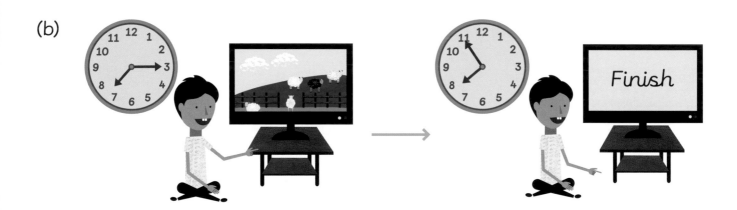

(c)

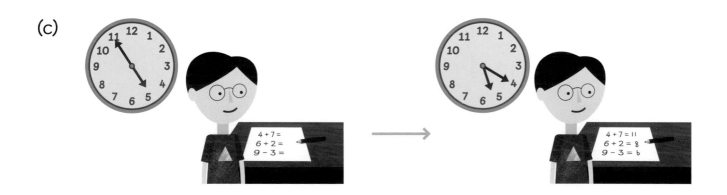

Complete Worksheet **6** – Page **139 – 140**

Finding Ending Times

In Focus

Elliott's favourite show starts in 2 hours.
Amira's favourite show starts in 30 minutes.
What times do their favourite shows start?

Let's Learn

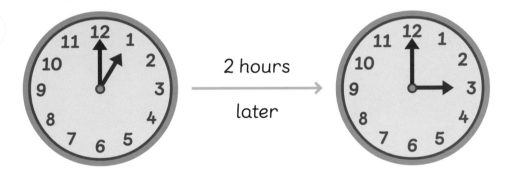

3:00 is 2 hours after 1:00.
Elliott's favourite show starts at 3:00.

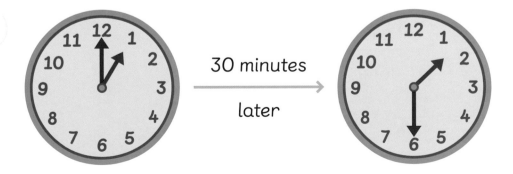

1:30 is 30 minutes after 1:00.
Amira's favourite show starts at 1:30.

3　What if it is 4:45 in the afternoon?
What time will it be 30 minutes from then?

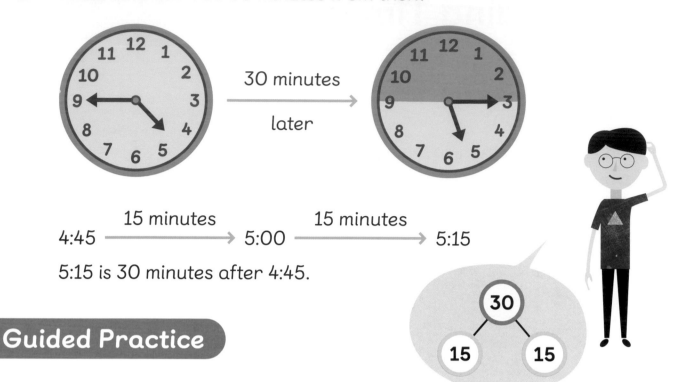

$$4:45 \xrightarrow{\text{15 minutes}} 5:00 \xrightarrow{\text{15 minutes}} 5:15$$

5:15 is 30 minutes after 4:45.

Guided Practice

Draw the clock hands.

1　(a)

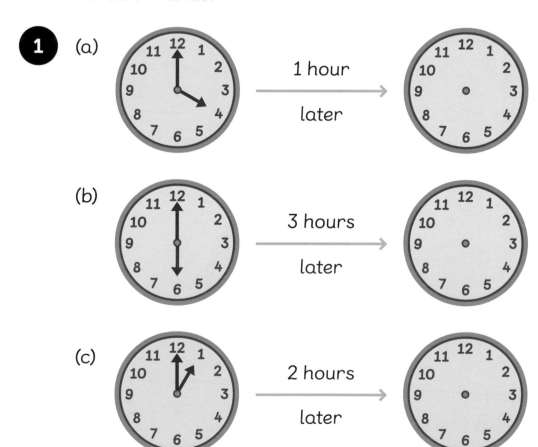

(b)　3 hours later

(c)　2 hours later

2 (a)
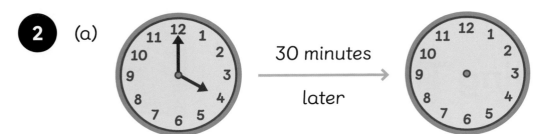

(b)

(c)
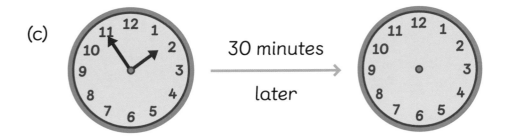

3 (a)

(b)
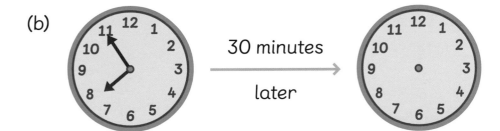

Suggest an activity that takes this long to complete.

Complete Worksheet **7** – Page **141 – 142**

Time

Finding Ending Times

In Focus

Emma's favourite cartoon
starts in 20 minutes.
It is a 35-minute show.
What time does the cartoon end?

Let's Learn

 1

 20 minutes

later

5:20 is 20 minutes after 5 o'clock.

2

 35 minutes

later

5:55 is 35 minutes after 5:20.
The cartoon ends at 5:55.

Can you tell what time
it will be 15 minutes
after 5:55?

5:55 is five minutes
to 6 o'clock.

Guided Practice

Draw the clock hands.

1 (a)  15 minutes later

(b)  55 minutes later

2 (a)  5 minutes later

(b)  25 minutes later

3 (a)

(b)

(c)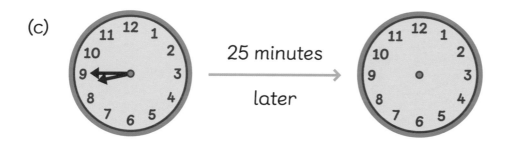

(d)

Complete Worksheet **8** – Page **143 – 144**

Finding Starting Times

In Focus

What time did the break start?

I just had my 30-minute break.

Let's Learn

1 What time was it 1 hour ago?

↗ 1 hour ago

It was 4 o'clock.

2 What time was it 30 minutes ago?

4 o'clock
half past 4
5 o'clock

↗

It was half past four.
The break started at 4:30.

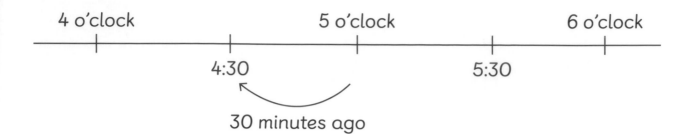

4 o'clock   5 o'clock   6 o'clock

4:30   5:30

30 minutes ago

Guided Practice

Draw the clock hands.

1 (a)

  1 hour later

(b)

  3 hours later

(c)

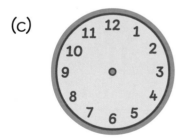 5 hours later

(d)

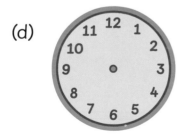 4 hours later

2 (a)

30 minutes

later

(b)

30 minutes

later

(c)

30 minutes

later

(d)

30 minutes

later

Complete Worksheet **9** – Page **145 – 146**

Finding Starting Times

In Focus

 arrive at

a restaurant at 6 o'clock for supper.

I left home an hour ago.

I left home 30 minutes ago.

Ruby

 Sam

Holly

I took 45 minutes to get here.

At what time did each of them leave home?

Let's Learn

1

 →

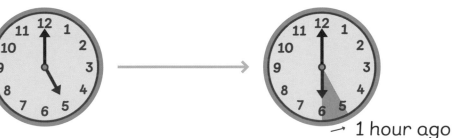

↪ 1 hour ago

An hour before 6 o'clock was 5 o'clock.

4 o'clock	5 o'clock	6 o'clock

1 hour ago

Ruby left home at 5 o'clock.

2

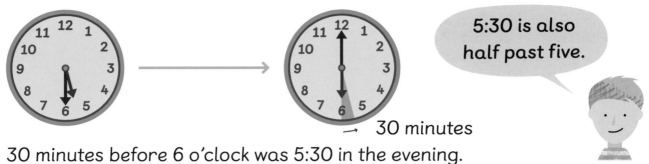

5:30 is also half past five.

30 minutes

30 minutes before 6 o'clock was 5:30 in the evening.

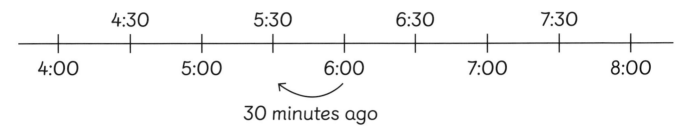

30 minutes ago

Sam left home at 5:30.

3

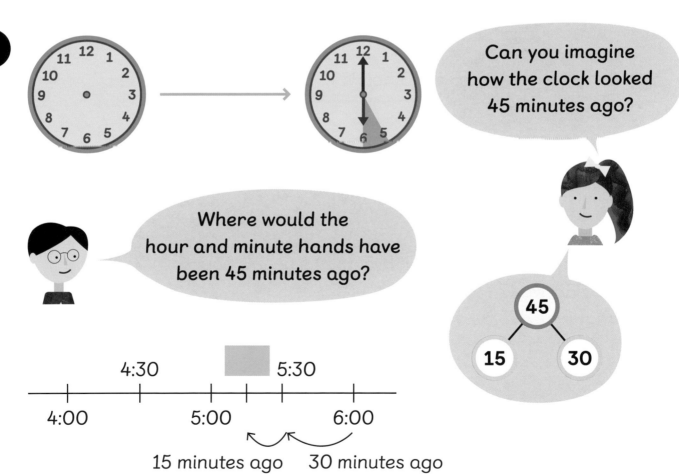

Can you imagine how the clock looked 45 minutes ago?

Where would the hour and minute hands have been 45 minutes ago?

45

15   30

15 minutes ago   30 minutes ago

45 minutes before 6 o'clock was 5:15 in the evening.
Holly left home at 5:15.

Guided Practice

Draw the clock hands.

1 (a)

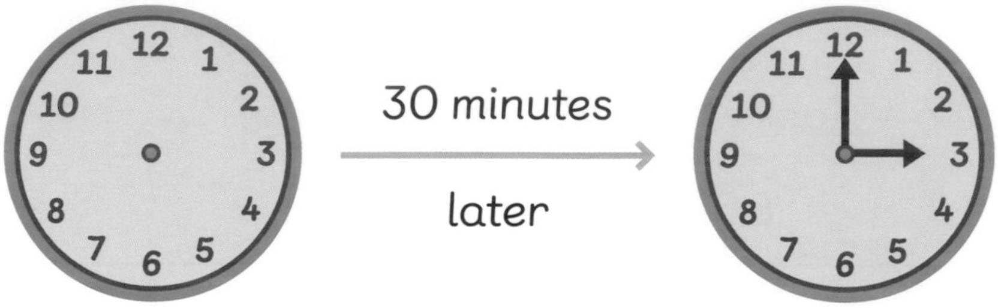
30 minutes
later

(b)

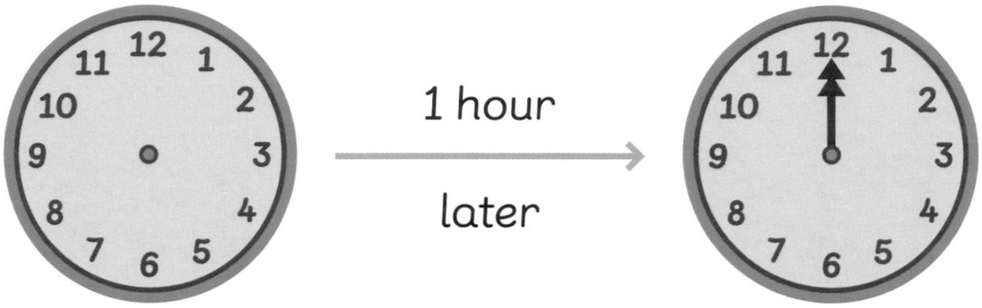
1 hour
later

(c)

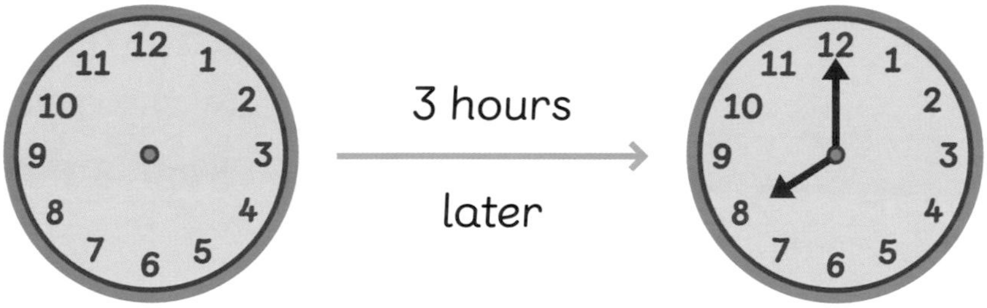
3 hours
later

2 Ruby took 55 minutes to travel to her gran's house.
Ruby arrived at 2 o'clock.
What time did Ruby start her journey?

3 Draw the clock hands.

(a)

20 minutes

later

(b)

20 minutes

later

4 Draw the clock hands.

(a)

20 minutes

later

(b)

35 minutes

later

Complete Worksheet **10** – Page **147 – 148**

Comparing Time

In Focus

playing football

eating supper

watching a movie

Which activity took the least time?
Which activity took the most time?

Let's Learn

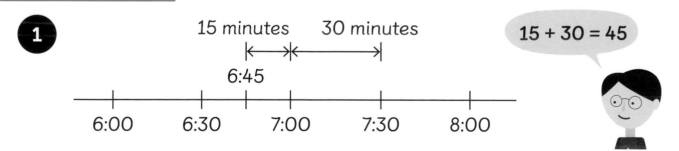

1

15 minutes   30 minutes

6:45

6:00   6:30   7:00   7:30   8:00

$15 + 30 = 45$

Playing football took 45 minutes.

2

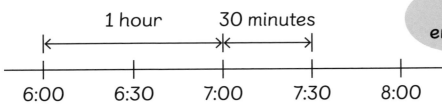

6:00   6:30   7:00   7:30   8:00

Having supper took 1 hour 30 minutes.

Football and supper ended at the same time.

But supper started first.

3

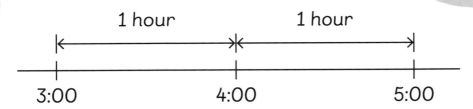

3:00   4:00   5:00

Watching a movie took [   ] hours.

[   ] took the least time.

[   ] took the most time.

Guided Practice

1 Which activity took more time?

badminton

hockey

[   ] took more time.

2 Who ran the fastest?
How many minutes did she take?

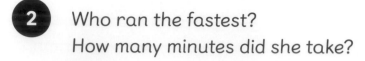

Lulu

Amira

Ruby

Lulu   Ruby
  Amira

[   ] ran the fastest.

She took [   ] minutes.

3 Which train journey took the longest?

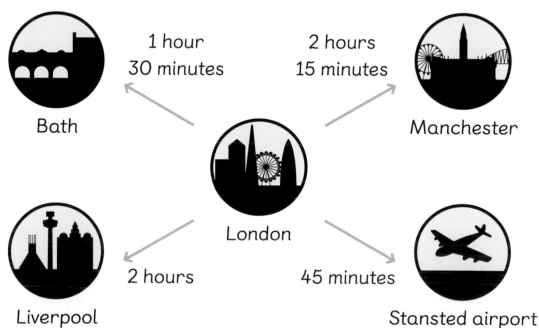

Bath

1 hour
30 minutes

2 hours
15 minutes

Manchester

London

Liverpool

2 hours

45 minutes

Stansted airport

The train journey from London to [   ] took the longest.

Complete Worksheet **11** – Page **149 – 150**

Amira arrived at a party at 2 o'clock in the afternoon.

Lulu arrived 1 hour after Amira.

Ruby arrived 1 hour after Lulu.

Sam arrived half an hour after Ruby.

Use  to help you.

The party started at 4 o'clock in the afternoon.
Are Amira, Lulu, Ruby and Sam on time?

What can you do in half an hour?

I can read [ ] pages of a storybook.

I can complete [ ] questions in my workbook.

I can run [ ] times around the school field.

How long is 30 minutes?

What can you do in 1 hour?

Self Check

I know how to...

☐ tell and write the time to 5 minutes.

☐ draw hands on a clock face to show time.

☐ find the duration of time.

☐ find the ending or starting time.

☐ compare and sequence intervals of time.

☐ know the number of minutes in an hour.

☐ know the number of hours in a day.

Which container has the most water?

Chapter 15
Volume

Comparing Volume

In Focus

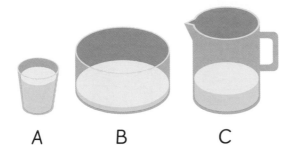

A   B   C

Compare the volume of water in the three containers.
Which container has the most water?

Let's Learn

Pour the water into identical containers.

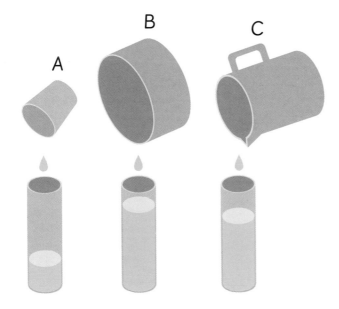

Look at the water levels and compare.

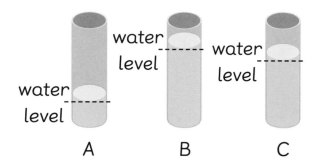

The volume of water in Container A is **less than** the volume of water in Container B.

The volume of water in Container B is **greater than** the volume of water in Container C.

Container A has the **least** amount of water.

We write 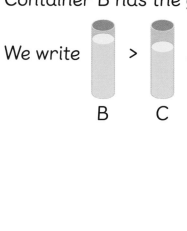 < .

Container A has less water than Container B.

Container B has the **greatest** amount of water.

We write  > .

Container B has more water than Container C.

Container B has the most water.

1 Cup A and Cup B have the same amount of water.
The water is poured into Container C and Container D.

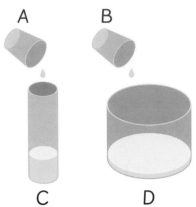

The volume of water in Container C is less than
the volume of water in Container D.   (true / false)

Use <, > or =.

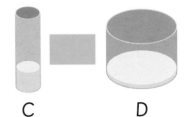

2 Compare the volume of water in the containers using
less, more, greatest or **least**.

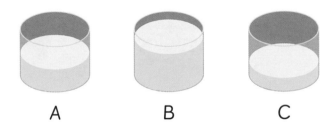

(a) Container A has ⬜ water than Container B.

(b) Container B has ⬜ water than Container C.

(c) Container C has the ⬜ amount of water.

(d) Container B has the ⬜ amount of water.

Also compare using <, > or =.

(e)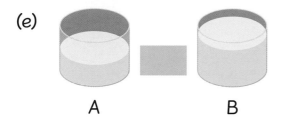
    A   B

(f)
    A   C

(g)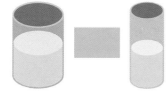
    B   C

3 Compare the volume of water in the 3 containers. Use <, > or =.

    A   B   C

(a)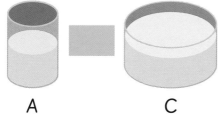
    A   B

(b)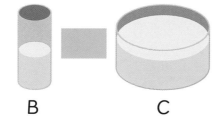
    A   C

(c)
    B   C

Complete Worksheet **1** – Page **155 - 156**

Comparing Volume

In Focus

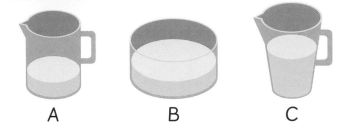

A   B   C

Compare the volume of water in the three containers.
Which container has the most water?

Let's Learn

The water in Containers A, B and C is poured into cups of the same size.
Measure the volume of water in each container.

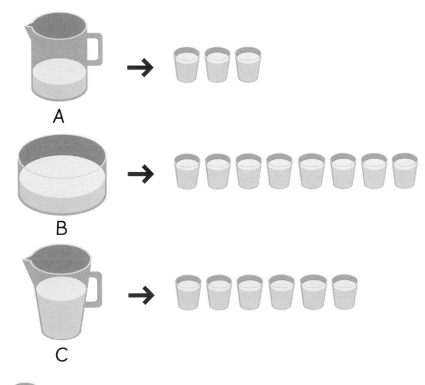

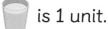 is 1 unit.

Volume of water in 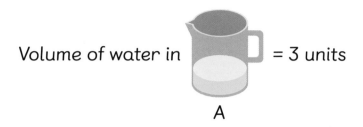 = 3 units

A

Volume of water in = 8 units.

B

Volume of water in = 6 units.

C

 contains the most water.

B

Work in groups of 3 to 4.

What you need:
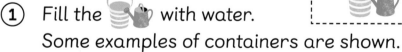

① Fill the with water.
Some examples of containers are shown.

② Which container do you think can hold more water? Why?

③ Find the capacity of the containers using .

Let = 1 unit.

All the water in the kettles is used to fill up the cups.

A

B

(a)   Kettle [ ] has less water than Kettle [ ].

(b)   Which kettle has a greater amount of water? Kettle [ ].

(c)   Use <, > or =.

A   B

Complete Worksheet **2** – Page **157 - 158**

Measuring Volume in Litres

In Focus

Amira bought these from the shop.
How much liquid is there in each container?

Let's Learn

We can measure volume with this 1-litre beaker.

Pour the mineral water from the bottle into a beaker.

The volume of water is about 1 litre.
The **litre** is a unit of volume.
We write **l** for litre.

The volume of cooking oil is more than 1 l.

The volume of cooking oil is about ▢ l.

3 Pour some juice into a glass.

The glass contains less than 1 l of juice.

4 Is the volume of water in the jug more or less than 1 l?
Use the 1-litre beaker to measure.

The jug contains ▢ than 1 l of water.

Work in groups of 4.

What you need:

① Some examples of containers are shown.

② Guess the volume of water in each container.
Is the volume **more than**, **less than** or **about** 1 l?
If you guess more than 1 l, what do you think is the actual volume?

③ Use to fill the with water and check your guess.

Count the number of bottles used to fill the containers.

④ Complete the table.

container	my guess (more than, less than or about 1 l)	measured volume

1 Compare using **more** or **less**.

(a)

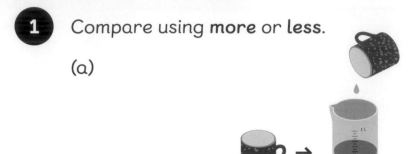

The volume of tea in the cup is ⬚⬚⬚⬚⬚ than 1 l.

(b)

The pot contains ⬚⬚⬚⬚⬚ than 1 l of coffee.

2 Pour all the washing liquid into 1-litre beakers.

The volume of washing liquid is ⬚⬚ l.

3 Which bottles will you use to fill up the bucket completely?

1 l   2 l   2 l   2 l   6 l

Complete Worksheet 3 – Page 159 – 161

Measuring Volume in Millilitres

In Focus

Lulu collects soap containers from different hotels.

How many bottles can 1 l of water fill?

Let's Learn

1 The bottle holds 20 millilitres of liquid.

1 litre of water can fill about 50 bottles like this one.

2

 We can measure volume with this measuring beaker.

The volume is 20 millilitres.
We write **ml** for millilitres.

20 millilitres is written like this.

20 ml

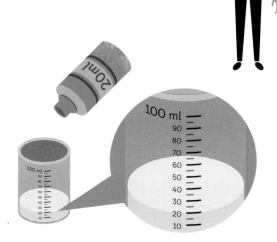

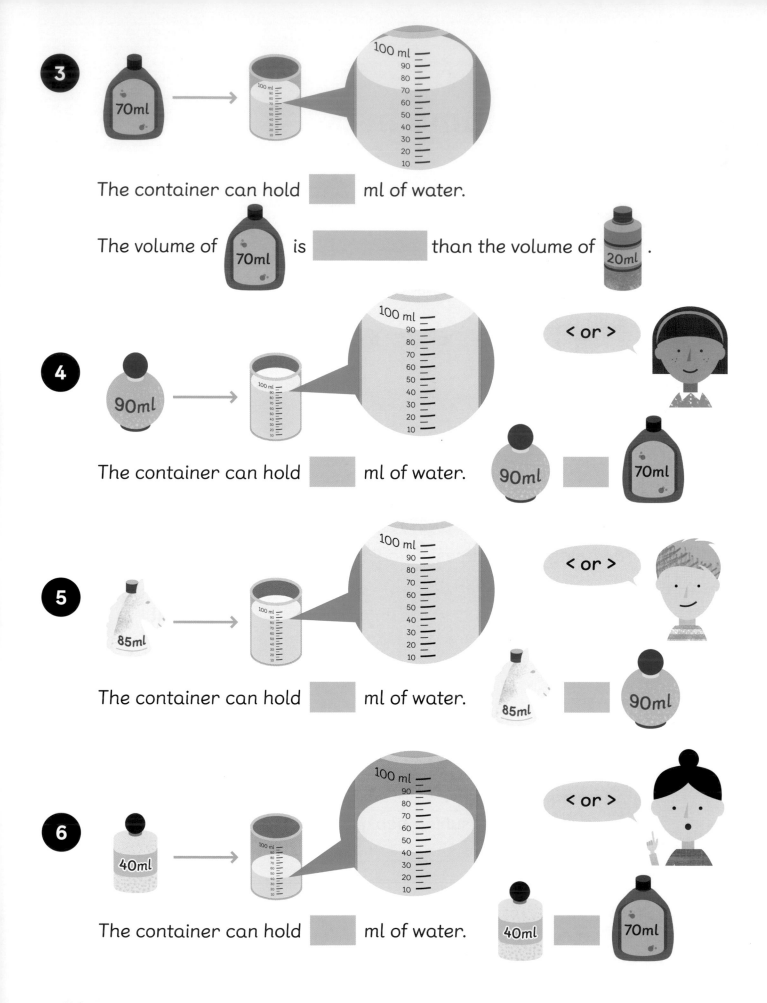

3

The container can hold [ ] ml of water.

The volume of 70ml is [ ] than the volume of 20ml .

4

< or >

The container can hold [ ] ml of water.

90ml [ ] 70ml

5

< or >

The container can hold [ ] ml of water.

85ml [ ] 90ml

6

< or >

The container can hold [ ] ml of water.

40ml [ ] 70ml

Guided Practice

Measure the volume of water.

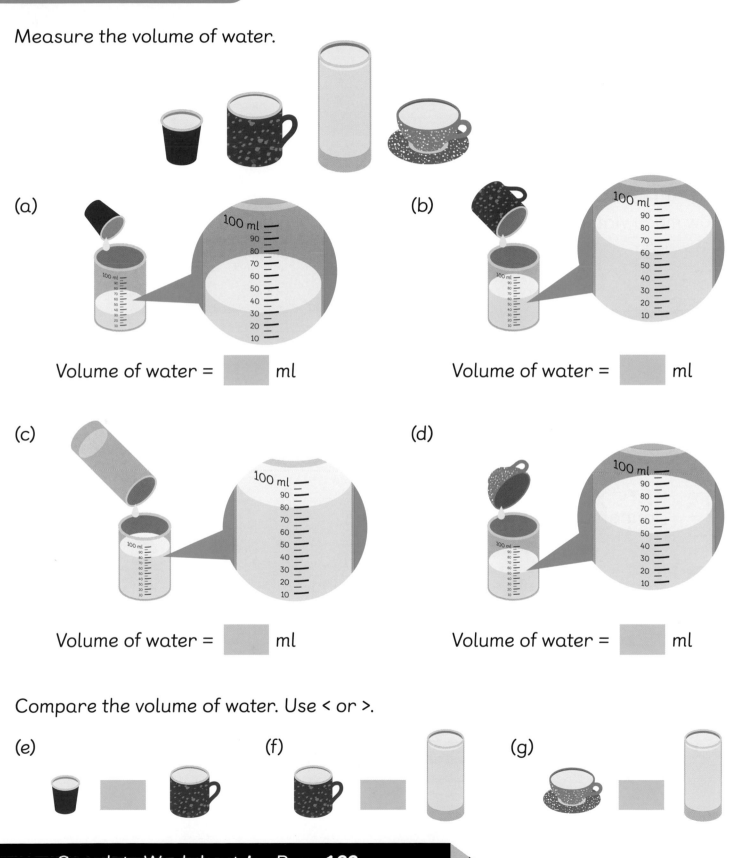

(a) Volume of water = ⬜ ml

(b) Volume of water = ⬜ ml

(c) Volume of water = ⬜ ml

(d) Volume of water = ⬜ ml

Compare the volume of water. Use < or >.

(e) ⬜

(f) ⬜

(g) ⬜

Complete Worksheet 4 – Page **162**

Solving Word Problems

In Focus

Hannah washed her vegetables and fruit.
How much water did she use altogether?

3 l   2 l

Let's Learn

1 Hannah used 3 l of water to wash the fruit.
She used 2 l of water to wash vegetables.
How much water did she use altogether?

3 + 2 = 5
Hannah used 5 l of water altogether.

2 A car had 30 l of petrol at the beginning.
After being driven for some time,
the car had 12 l of petrol left.
How much petrol did the car use?

You can draw a model to help you.

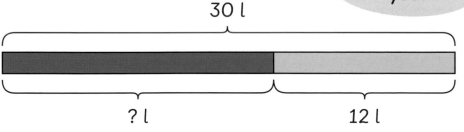

30 l

? l   12 l

30 − 12 = 18
The car used 18 l of petrol.

Solve.

1 There is 45 l of water in a fish tank.
The fish tank has a crack and 18 l of water leaks out.
How much water is left in the fish tank?

2 A petrol tank can hold 50 l of petrol.
There is 12 l of petrol in the tank.
How many more litres of petrol is needed to fill the tank completely?

3 Holly makes some lemonade to sell.
She mixes 4 l of lemon juice, 5 l of sugar syrup and 17 l of water.
How many litres of lemonade does she make?

Complete Worksheet 5 – Page 163 - 164

Solving Word Problems

In Focus

 can hold 22 ml more water than .

How much water can hold?

Let's Learn

1 had 85 ml of water.

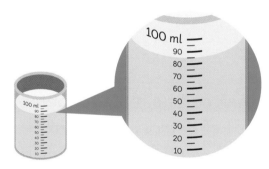

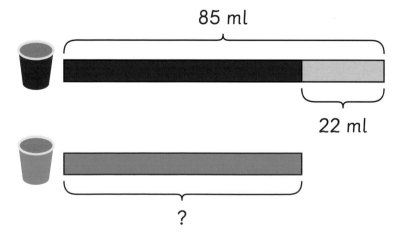

$85 - 22 = 63$

 can hold 63 ml of water.

The capacity of 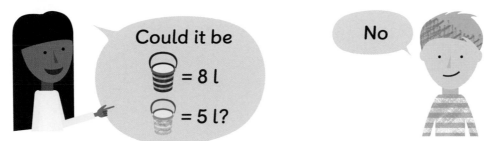 is 3 l less than the capacity of .

The two buckets can hold 11 l of water.

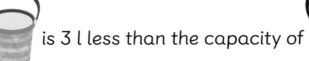

Could it be

= 8 l

= 5 l?

No

11 − 3 = 8

3 l

11 l

8 l

4 + 4 = 8

has a capacity of 4 l.

has a capacity of 7 l.

Guided Practice

Container A has 25 l of cooking oil.
Container B has 9 l more cooking oil than Container A.

(a)   What is the volume of cooking oil in Container B?

(b)   How much cooking oil is there altogether?

Complete Worksheet **6** – Page **165 - 167**

Solving Word Problems

In Focus

How much water did Ravi use to water the plants?

Let's Learn

1 Ravi used 5 buckets of water to water the plants.
Each bucket contained 4 l of water.
How much water did he use?

$5 \times 4 = 20$

Ravi used 20 l of water.

Read the problem.
Do we multiply or
divide?

2 Ruby pours 10 l of apple juice equally into 5 bottles.
How many litres of apple juice does each bottle contain?

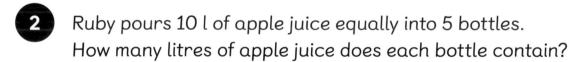

Each bottle contains [ ] l of apple juice.

Guided Practice

Solve.

1 Emma bought 8 bottles of liquid soap.
Each bottle contains 2 l of liquid soap.
How many litres of liquid soap did she buy?

2 Charles prepares 10 l of fruit punch for his birthday party.
He pours the fruit punch equally into 2 bottles.
How much fruit punch is there in each bottle?

Complete Worksheet 7 – Page 168 – 169

Mind Workout

Elliott needs to fill an empty bucket with 7 l of water.

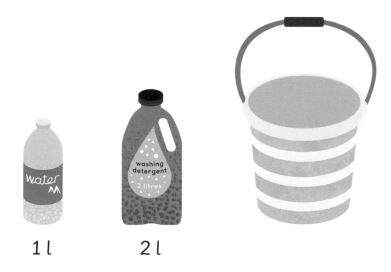

1 l   2 l

How can he use the containers to fill the bucket?

Find and cut out pictures of containers from newspapers or magazines.

Can each container hold more than, less than or about 1 litre of water?

I know how to...

☐ compare volume.

☐ measure volume in litres (l) and millilitres (ml)

☐ solve word problems on volume.